A wonderful work, with amazing clarity, honesty, and an openness to reality. I felt an overflow of love in many of the ideas offered by Farnaz Masumian. I have no doubt that the variety of meditation practices and visualization techniques contained in this book will nourish the hearts and minds of all kinds of readers.

Nader Saiedi, author of *Gate of the Heart*

This is tomato bisque for the soul, where the reader can actually sample meditation techniques – drawn from the great masters and contemplative traditions of world religions. Here, the reader can taste the physiological, psychological and spiritual benefits of meditation . . . the author shows how these techniques, done singly or in combination, promote *peace of mind, comfort, confidence, strength, wisdom and* self-empowerment for the benefit of self and others – all with scientific evidence of meditation's powers to uplift body and mind. Professor Masumian authenticates her meditation handbook by sharing what she herself has experienced while performing these various meditations – a consummate personal touch. A gift by a gifted author.

Christopher Buck, author of *Religions Myths and Visions of America*

ABOUT THE AUTHOR

Farnaz Masumian has been teaching world religions at institutions of higher education since 1992, including the University of Texas at Austin since 2005. Her primary research interests are in the areas of life after death, near-death experiences (NDEs), and meditation. Among her publications are several books, including *Life after Death: A Study of the Afterlife in World Religions* (Oneworld Publications, 1995, reprinted in 2002 by Kalimát Press), and *Divine Educators* (George Ronald, 2005), which she co-authored with her husband, Bijan Masumian. *Life After Death* has so far been translated into Russian, Polish, and Indonesian languages and won first prize in the religion/spirituality category at the 1998 Beijing, China Book Fair.

THE DIVINE ART OF MEDITATION

The Divine Art of Meditation

Meditation and visualization techniques for
a healthy mind, body and soul

Farnaz Masumian

GEORGE RONALD OXFORD

George Ronald Publisher
Oxford
www.grbooks.com

A catalogue record for this book in available
from the British Library

ISBN 978–0–85398–586–0

Cover Design: Steiner Graphics

O friend, the heart is the dwelling of eternal mysteries, make it not the home of fleeting fancies; waste not the treasure of thy precious life in employment with this swiftly passing world. Thou comest from the world of holiness – bind not thine heart to the earth; thou art a dweller in the court of nearness – choose not the homeland of the dust.

Bahá'u'lláh

I now assure thee, O servant of God, that, if thy mind become empty and pure from every mention and thought and thy heart attracted wholly to the Kingdom of God, forget all else besides God and come in communion with the Spirit of God, then the Holy Spirit will assist thee with a power which will enable thee to penetrate all things, and a Dazzling Spark which enlightens all sides, a Brilliant Flame in the zenith of the heavens, will teach thee that which thou dost not know of the facts of the universe and of the divine doctrine.

'Abdu'l-Bahá

This book is dedicated to all my 'angels'

especially Dr 'Alímorad Dávudí
my beloved teacher who gave up his life for the cause of world peace
and brotherhood;

the late Dr Daniel Jordan
whose insight into the Word of God made a profound impact on
my spiritual journey;

and my late cousin, Golnar Rafi'i (Sahba)
whose life of service has been a great source of inspiration to me

CONTENTS

NOTES AND ACKNOWLEDGEMENTS

No specific forms of meditation are prescribed in the Bahá'í Faith. Bahá'ís are, however, enjoined to meditate, as will be clear from this book. The suggestions given here are drawn from the experience of the many millions of people who have learned how to meditate in past centuries, as well as from my own personal experience and that of the increasing numbers of people who are learning today. It should be emphasized that none of these methods are part of the Bahá'í teachings or particularly recommended for believers, who are free to carry out their religious obligation to meditate in any manner they prefer.

In quoting from the Sacred Texts of earlier religions, I have used Juan Mascaro's translations of the Dhammapada and the Bhagavad Gita, Nyanasatta Thera's translation of the Sattipatthana Sutta, the King James and the Revised Standard Version of the Holy Bible, and Muhammad Asad's and Rodwell's translations of the Holy Qur'án.

I would like to thank my husband Bijan Masumian for his research and valuable contributions to Chapter 4, 'The Scientific Evidence', as well as for editing the manuscript. I am also grateful to our son Adib Masumian who encouraged me to write this book and also served as a second editor. Both Bijan and Adib have made significant improvements to the content and quality of this work.

Farnaz Masumian
September 2014

PREFACE

Your thoughts are a veil on the face of the Moon.
That Moon is your heart, and those thoughts cover your heart.
So let them go, just let them fall into the water.

Rumi [1]

Today, the word meditation usually conjures up images of a person deep in concentration, sitting on a mat cross-legged with eyes closed. Yet every day, countless millions across the world engage in the practice in a wide variety of forms and postures. While the concept and practice of meditation is generally believed to have originated in Hindu scriptures some 5,000 years ago, it is the founder of Buddhism, Gautama Buddha – himself originally a Hindu – who is usually credited with popularizing the practice in the modern world. [2] The most dramatic moment in Buddha's life, his enlightenment, took place during a meditation session, cross-legged under a Bodhi tree, much in the same posture that millions of Buddhists and non-Buddhists around the world now emulate every day.

The roots of western-style meditation go back to Greek and Egyptian mystery religions as well as aboriginal and Native American religious traditions. However, meditation in the western hemisphere first became popularized mostly through the Abrahamic religions – Judaism, Christianity and Islam – where for centuries hundreds of millions of adherents have engaged in prayer, reflection or contemplation in synagogues, churches, monasteries, mosques and other places of worship. In more recent times, the practice became particularly attractive in North America in the 1960s and 1970s thanks to the attention it received from pop icons like the Beatles, who became interested in Transcendental Meditation (TM).[3] At first, many scientists and medical doctors were sceptical of any potential health benefits from meditation. However, with growing popularity of the practice in North America and Europe, particularly among the young, the medical and scientific communities began to pay closer attention to the phenomenon and started conducting research on its potential health benefits.

Today, thanks to state-of-the-art medical equipment such as fMRI[4] (Functional Magnetic Resonance Imagery) and EEG[5] (Electroencephalography), we have a growing body of scientific evidence that meditation can lead to significant changes in the human body.[6] A good example of such studies are the experiments by American cardiologist Dr Herbert Benson, which documented the positive effects of meditation on the human mind and body in a book titled *The Breakout Principle,* a sequel to his classic work *The Relaxation Response.* Benson is a graduate of the Harvard School of Medicine and author or co-author of more than 175 scientific publications and 11 books. Over four million copies of his books have been sold. He is also the founder of the Mind/Body Medical Institute and is one of the first western physicians to bring spirituality and healing into mainstream medicine. In the Foreword to the revised 2000 version of *The Relaxation Response,* first published in 1974, Benson notes the following:

> Indeed, the world today is dramatically different from the world that was first introduced to the connections of mind and body detailed in *The Relaxation Response.* Three decades ago, it was considered scientific heresy for a Harvard physician and researcher to hypothesize that stress contributed to health problems and to publish studies showing that mental focusing techniques were good for the body. I broke ranks with the medical establishment when I decided to pursue this theory and to prove or disprove it in my medical research.
>
> Today we, as a society, take for granted the multifaceted and intimate relationship between mind and body. Scientists

now avidly pursue ties between brain activity and physical manifestations. Millions of Americans now elicit the Relaxation Response regularly, as Yoga classes swell, athletes report 'being in the Zone', and people set up quiet places in their homes to meditate or pray.

So much has changed: our economy is becoming more globalized, and barriers between countries are being pulled down. But we have yet to witness a corollary paradigm shift in medicine. Today, our appetites have been whetted with quick fixes, so much so that our quest for diagnostic gadgets and miracle drugs has almost overcome common sense. We expect that surgical acumen will be enough to save us and if not, the next remarkable scientific discovery will. Although mind/body therapies have been proven effective for the vast majority of every-day medical problems, we are still far more apt to run to our medicine cabinet to relieve aches and pains than to consider relaxation or stress-management techniques. [7]

Benson goes on to note that even when we don't exercise regularly or get a good night's sleep – and despite the fact that many of us bombard our bodies with stress and fatty food – our bodies remain incredibly reliable. Yet, instead of giving them a chance to heal themselves through their internal mechanisms, we are quick to seek out chemicals and run to medical and surgical procedures at a whim. Over 40 years of research by Benson and other scientists have now demonstrated the physiological, psychological, and spiritual benefits of meditation and relaxation. See Chapter 4 on 'The Scientific Evidence' for more on the health benefits of meditation.

Why This Book?

Many books have been written on meditation and its benefits. But few have dealt with the healing impact of the practice on the life of the author, who happens to be my wife of 35 years. Also, this book provides unique meditational practices not found elsewhere.

These methods have been of great help in her long journey to physical, mental and spiritual peace and serenity. Farnaz has been a lecturer in world religions at institutions of higher education since 1992. She is currently teaching a class on world religions and social work at the University of Texas at Austin. Her background has enabled her to draw inspiration for this work primarily from the sacred literature of the world. Her thinking and methods are also influenced by such spiritual figures as Brother Lawrence, a 17th-century Christian monk who served at the Carmelite monastery in Paris (see chapter 9); Mahatma Gandhi (see chapter 11), and numerous others (see chapter 19).

A final word: if you have a sceptical mind, like me, which puts prime value on scientific evidence, you might want to read the chapter on 'The Scientific Evidence' first. Either way, I think most readers will find this work both inspiring and practical. As someone who started with doubts but is now a meditation practitioner himself, I can tell you that I have. But you need to read the book and decide for yourself.

Bijan Masumian, PhD
September 2014

PART I

MEDITATION FOR THE 21ST CENTURY

For him who has conquered the mind, the mind is the best
of friends; but for one who has failed to do so, his mind will
remain the greatest enemy.

Bhagavad Gita 6:6

Today, the practice of meditation is becoming increasingly
common among people from all walks of life. More of us are
being introduced to the benefits of meditation which has been
cherished and practised since ancient times. It is encouraged in
high-level corporate sessions, during coffee breaks, before aca-
demic tests, and prior to athletic competition.[1] During a speech
at Harvard University, the Dalai Lama said the following on the
significance of meditation:

> In this century, human knowledge is extremely expanded and
> developed but this is mainly knowledge of the external world
> . . . We spend a large amount of the best human brain power
> looking outside – too much, and it seems we do not spend
> adequate effort to look within, to think inwardly . . . Perhaps

now that the Western sciences have reached down into the atom and out into the cosmos finally to realize the extreme vulnerability of all life and value, it is becoming credible, even obvious, that the Inner Science is of supreme importance. Certainly physics designed the bombs, biology, the germ warfare, chemistry, the nerve gas, and so on, but it will be the unhealthy emotions of individuals that will trigger these horrors. These emotions can only be controlled, reshaped, and rechanneled by technologies developed from successful Inner Science.[2]

Similar sentiments have been echoed in the following words of the Lakota holy man Black Elk:

There can never be peace between nations until we know the true peace which is in the souls of men. This comes when men realize their oneness with the universe and all its powers, and that the Great Spirit is at its center; that all things are his works, and that this center is really everywhere. It is within each of us.[3]

1
INTRODUCTION

What we are today comes from our thoughts of yesterday, and our present thoughts build our life of tomorrow: our life is the creation of our mind. If a man speaks or acts with an impure mind, suffering follows him as the wheel of the cart follows the beast that draws the cart.

Dhammapada 1:1

Today, many of us seem to live our lives like honeybees collecting honey which, at the end, we will leave to others for their enjoyment! Our values are often twisted. Our success is largely measured by the size of our bank account, how beautiful or handsome we are, or how luxurious are our homes, cars or boats. Reality TV shows continue to appeal to millions of us who choose to live vicariously through others, rather than taking charge of our own lives and focusing on manifesting the hidden treasures that are invested in our souls.

Women are often encouraged to seek superficial and temporary beauty, at the risk of endangering their health, even killing themselves,[1] while men are encouraged to appreciate and chase a life of pleasure. In contrast, those whose lives are centred on spirituality are frequently ridiculed as old-fashioned or at least looked down upon. We seek surgical procedures to fight the natural ageing process and enjoy 'borrowed youth' a bit longer, even though we know, deep in our hearts, that it is ultimately a losing battle. We can upgrade our homes, go from a boat to a yacht, and maybe even own a private jet. Yet, in the end, we will have to leave all these material possessions behind. We can't take anything with us to 'the other side', even if we try, like the Pennsylvania man who asked to be buried with his beloved Corvette![2]

So, are there other paths, lifestyles or value systems to consider? Of course, there are plenty. I suggest one alternative here: a meditative life centred on God, which means to have Him in mind in our thoughts, words and deeds as much as we humanly can. And that is where 'God-centred meditation' comes in. Simply put, God plays the central role in my perspective on life and in my meditation philosophy and techniques. I believe that unless we connect to God through His Name and His life-giving, transformative Word found in the primary sources of the world's great religions, we will not experience *true, lasting* joy and peace in life. Enduring happiness comes from within when we nurture and strengthen the divine side in us, attempt to live a spiritual life, and connect to our Creator. This can happen by living a God-centred life: engaging in prayer and meditation, and immersing ourselves in the ocean of God's Words. At the core of this approach to life is the human heart. In many religious traditions, the human heart is characterized as God's home or throne. For instance, in *The Hidden Words of Bahá'u'lláh* we read:

> Thy heart is My home; sanctify it for My descent. Thy spirit is My place of revelation; cleanse it for My manifestation.[3]

A similar idea can be seen in the Bhagavad Gita:

> . . . thy God dwells in thy heart. [4]

While in the Bible the Psalmist said:

> God is the strength of my heart and my portion forever. [5]

In a Muslim hadith,[6] we read:

> Neither My earth, nor My heaven can contain Me. Indeed it is the heart of the man of faith which can contain Me. [7]

Therefore, the first and most crucial step in living a God-centred life is to prepare the 'home' for the Beloved by purifying our heart through prayer, meditation and a practice called *zikr*[8] in Sufism and *mantra*[9] in Hinduism. The sanctification of the heart will, in turn, make our souls more susceptible to receiving divine inspiration and confirmation, which will reinforce living a God-centred life:

> Wherefore, a man should make ready his heart that it be worthy of the descent of heavenly grace, and that the bounteous Cup-Bearer may give him to drink of the wine of bestowal from the merciful vessel.[10]

The same idea is echoed in the following passage from 'Abdu'l-Bahá:

> Then know, O thou virtuous soul, that as soon as thou becomest separated from aught else save God and dost cut thyself from the worldly things, thy heart will shine with lights of divinity and with the effulgence of the Sun of Truth from the horizon of the Realm of Might, and then thou wilt be filled by the spirit of power from God and become capable of doing that which thou desirest. This is the confirmed truth.[11]

In addition, certain types of meditation such as reflective meditation or contemplation on the sacred text can also lead to spiritual transformation by giving us insights into deeper meanings of the sacred Word. In the following passage, Bahá'u'lláh exhorts His followers to immerse themselves in the ocean of His Writings to find pearls of great value in the depth of this vast ocean. Immersion, by definition, necessitates a deeper dive, which implies reflection or contemplation:

> O My servants! My holy, My divinely ordained Revelation may be likened unto an ocean in whose depths are concealed innumerable pearls of great price, of surpassing lustre. It is the duty of every seeker to bestir himself and strive to attain

the shores of this ocean, so that he may, in proportion to the eagerness of his search and the efforts he hath exerted, partake of such benefits as have been pre-ordained in God's irrevocable and hidden Tablets . . . The one true God is My witness! This most great, this fathomless and surging Ocean is near, astonishingly near, unto you. Behold it is closer to you than your life-vein! Swift as the twinkling of an eye ye can, if ye but wish it, reach and partake of this imperishable favour, this God-given grace, this incorruptible gift, this most potent and unspeakably glorious bounty.[12]

If you believe in a Supreme Being and are open to the idea of God-centred meditation, you will probably find many suggested practices in this book valuable, including mantra meditation, healing meditation, and contemplation on the holy texts. However, even if you don't believe in God, there is plenty of content and techniques you may find quite useful: the purpose of meditation, the significant amount of scientific data gathered from a variety of sources in support of the physiological and psychological benefits of meditation, a wide array of meditation techniques that are not God-centred such as single object meditation, Vipassana meditation, metta meditation, gratitude meditation, and music meditation as well as unique visualization techniques that could prove beneficial in your journey to health, happiness and peace of mind.

This book also provides new daily meditation and visualization practices that are not found in other sources, such as
- Suggested daily meditation and visualization
- Visualization for overcoming negative thoughts and emotions
- Bedtime visualization
- Creating an evening oasis

Now, let's move on to the content of the book, beginning with the definition of meditation.

2
WHAT IS MEDITATION?

Considering that this body is frail like a jar, make your mind strong like a fortress and fight the great fight against MARA, all evil temptations. After victory guard well your conquests, and ever for ever watch.

Dhammapada 3:40

Meditation is the skill of paying attention and developing concentration of mind. When our mind learns to focus on an object of meditation without wavering, we will enjoy a relaxed mind and a calm body.[1]

A great misunderstanding about meditation is that its purpose is to make our minds blank as we sit in an uncomfortable position. In reality, meditation is a practice in which we try to substitute our thoughts with another object of attention such as a mantra, a candle flame, a leaf, breath, and the like. When our minds become absorbed in something other than our thoughts, they become relaxed. Relaxation is one of the many benefits of meditation. Meditation can also be viewed as a procedure for working with our mind. Just as exercise can lead to a fit body, meditation can lead to obtaining a sound and wholesome mind.[2]

Wendi Momen identifies a range of possibilities as goals for meditation:

For some, meditation is a way of realizing, or actualizing, one's true nature. For others, the purpose of meditation is to achieve a sense of unity with the universe or a higher sense of one's place in it. Others meditate to attain 'enlightenment' or 'illumination'; for some, this enlightenment comes from within oneself while others believe it to be external to the person, stemming from the divine or perhaps the universe itself. Some seek 'the light within' the spark of the divine in man. Others seek spiritual ecstasy or 'rapturous love'.[3]

The practice of meditation is ancient and has been present in all major human cultures:

> Meditation is not something that was invented in – and happened in – history. It is an ageless human experience that has been discovered and explored and used in every period and every culture that we know about. It has always been used by only a few in each place and time, but for those few who have worked seriously at it there has been real gain. It has brought them increased ability to function and find peace and joy.[4]

Meditation techniques have been mostly developed by mystics in different mystical traditions of various cultures.[5] Meditation can also be defined as thought that is directed by our will.[6] One of the most significant goals of meditation is self-mastery. Over the years, as meditation becomes an indispensable part of our lives and our meditation practice deepens, we will be able to control our thoughts and actions. We will refuse to think about a subject or act in a manner we don't want to. This is a highly empowering, liberating and rewarding experience. However, the loftiest goal of meditation is to have an experience of God.[7]

Why Do We Need to Meditate?

> Invisible and subtle is the mind, and it flies after fancies wherever it likes; but let the wise man guard well his mind, for a mind well guarded is a source of great joy.[8]

The fundamental goal of meditation is to help us liberate our conscious mind from the grasp of our automatic random thoughts:

Most people believe that they think, when in fact their thoughts merely occur. What is more, there is no control over these random thoughts, and even more calamitous, to a degree these thoughts control them. The declaration . . . I think therefore I am – is not quite accurate. We are not because we think; rather we are what our reactive thinking invents us to be. This automaticity can be a tyrant, and the quest is to liberate ourselves from it. A prevailing objective of meditation is to have hegemony over one's thoughts. A person meditates to experience controlled thinking, which simply put, is to master one's thoughts and retain the ability to consciously decide what one will think about, and for how long that thought will be maintained.[9]

There is stillness beneath all the chatter of our mind.[10] Meditation can help us access this inner place of stillness, and transform our minds from a state of confusion, restlessness, unease and disharmony to a state of peace, rest, calm and harmony. It is not the aim of meditation to have supernatural experiences such as seeing various colours, bright lights, or visions of people talking to us. Neither should we adopt the practice of meditation to help us get 'high'. On the contrary, such distracting experiences lead to mental agitation and disquiet and therefore prevent us from a very significant goal of meditation: the attainment of peace and tranquillity.

To understand the effects of meditation, we need to familiarize ourselves with the workings of the mind. We can think of an ordinary mind as a turbulent lake. The surface of this lake is formed by a flow of continuous waves of concerns, anxieties, worries, fears, dreams and regrets, which can prevent us from experiencing a life of happiness and serenity. Psychologists refer to the flow of our thoughts as a chain of associations. One thought triggers the next thought which, in turn, is connected to still another thought and so on. Thus a string of connected thoughts constantly runs through our mind, leaving us with confusion or even mental fatigue. Meditation is our best ally in breaking the chain of associations and providing us with a calm and centred mind.[11]

For instance, as we are meditating, the thought of our favourite food may arise in our mind and make us lose our focus for some time. Soon, this seemingly pleasant thought can carry us away to other related thoughts. We may remember that we have not done our grocery shopping and ultimately to worrying about how we can fit shopping into our schedule. On the other hand, when we do not focus on the thought of food as it arises during meditation, and bring our mind gently back to the object of our meditation, we can gradually discipline our mind to listen to us even when we are not meditating. Thus, little by little, meditation and its allied practices will help us gain mastery over our mind. This can, in turn, lead to a life of peace and serenity.

Furthermore, meditation can help us manifest such inner qualities as wisdom, creativity, peacefulness, patience, love and a host of other virtues that are latent within our souls.[12] Today, thanks to decades of research which started with pioneers such as Herbert Benson of Harvard University, we have plenty of research from the medical community that provides compelling reasons why we should meditate.

Many people, especially the religious, practise meditation because they feel that faith and the mystical need to establish a bond with the Creator are intertwined. Prayer and meditation play fundamental roles in establishing and nurturing this bond. For the religious, the key to understanding why we need to meditate is to recognize the central role of meditation in the sanctification of the human heart which, to them, is one of the primary goals of our existence.

3

MEDITATION AND THE BAHÁ'Í FAITH

The bestowal of the Spirit is given in reflection and meditation.
'Abdu'l-Bahá [1]

In the Bahá'í Faith, as in many other world religions, the purpose of meditation is to purify our hearts and to help us draw closer to God. 'Abdu'l-Bahá said, 'Nearness is likeness.'[2] So, the closer we draw to God, the more God-like we become:

The core of religious faith is that mystic feeling that unites man with God. This state of spiritual communion can be brought about and maintained by means of meditation and prayer.[3]

No less essential to nourishing this vitality [of faith] is the cultivation of a sense of spirituality, that mystic feeling which unites the individual with God and is achieved through meditation and prayer.[4]

From the Bahá'í perspective, the key to understanding why we need to meditate is to recognize the central role of meditation in the sanctification of the human heart, which is one of the primary goals of our existence. For example, the Bahá'í scriptures use the analogy of the sun and the mirror to help explain how prayer and meditation can help remove the dust of worldliness from the mirror of our heart so that the heart can faithfully reflect the divine light that is hidden in our innermost reality:

Man possesses two kinds of susceptibilities: the natural emotions, which are like dust upon the mirror, and spiritual susceptibilities, which are merciful and heavenly characteristics.

There is a power which purifies the mirror from dust and transforms its reflection into intense brilliancy and radiance so that spiritual susceptibilities may chasten the hearts and heavenly bestowals sanctify them. What is the dust which obscures the mirror? It is attachment to the world, avarice, envy, love of luxury and comfort, haughtiness and self-desire; this is the dust which prevents reflection of the rays of the Sun of Reality in the mirror. The natural emotions are blameworthy and are like rust which deprives the heart of the bounties of God. But sincerity, justice, humility, severance, and love for the believers of God will purify the mirror and make it radiant with reflected rays from the Sun of Truth.[5]

Consider how a pure, well-polished mirror fully reflects the effulgence of the sun, no matter how distant the sun may be. As soon as the mirror is cleaned and purified, the sun will manifest itself. The more pure and sanctified the heart of man becomes, the nearer it draws to God, and the light of the Sun of Reality is revealed within it. This light sets hearts aglow with the fire of the love of God, opens in them the doors of knowledge and unseals the divine mysteries so that spiritual discoveries are made possible.[6]

These energies with which the Day Star of Divine bounty . . . hath endowed the reality of man lie, however, latent within him . . . The radiance of these energies may be obscured by worldly desires even as the light of the sun can be concealed beneath the dust and dross which cover the mirror.[7]

Therefore, the 'dust' and 'dross' that cover the mirrors of our hearts and prevent them from reflecting the divine light originate from our lower nature. By concentrating on a life of virtues characterized by prayer and meditation, we can gradually sanctify our heart so it can become a receptacle for divine light and guidance. 'Abdu'l-Bahá stresses the importance of being 'concentrated on a single point' as a means for attracting the divine light:

> O daughter of the Kingdom! Thy letter hath come and its contents make clear the fact that thou hast directed all thy thoughts toward acquiring light from the realms of mystery. So long as the thoughts of an individual are scattered he will achieve no results, but if his thinking be concentrated on a single point wonderful will be the fruits thereof.
>
> One cannot obtain the full force of the sunlight when it is cast on a flat mirror, but once the sun shineth upon a concave mirror, or on a lens that is convex, all its heat will be concentrated on a single point, and that one point will burn the hottest. Thus is it necessary to focus one's thinking on a single point so that it will become an effective force.[8]

Mirzá Abu'l-Faḍl, the renowned Bahá'í scholar, also elaborates on the role of concentration in spiritual growth:

> 'Abdu'l-Bahá said that there is in man a power of concentration not fully developed, which power rightly directed can lead him to great heights of knowledge, understanding and illumination. Prayer and supplication are the ladder, He said, 'by which the soul ascends and as the power of sustained communion with God develops the capacity to receive the influx of The Holy Spirit and to penetrate, the hidden mystery unfolds.' Prayer and communion is the only direct approach of the soul to God, and Bahá'u'lláh, the prophet founder of the Bahá'í Faith, has likened it unto 'a river of milk' which is the perfect nutriment, and the more we partake of this life-giving food, the more the soul shall advance in the path of God and the greater will be its progress.
>
> 'Abdu'l-Bahá, the son and successor of Bahá'u'lláh, has likened the power of concentration to a cubic crystal. He said, 'If you place a ruby, the hardest stone, in a seven times heated

furnace, the heat will have no effect, but if you place that ruby in a cubic crystal in the rays of the mid-day sun, it will be dissolved.' This, He has likened to the powers of concentration in man. He said, 'Whatsoever man concentrates upon, he will draw to himself.' Therefore in prayer and supplication he must close the door to all the outer world and turn his whole being to the Focal Point, the Manifestation of God in his day and thus draw into his soul the burning rays of the Sun of Truth, the Infinite Love, Light Beauty and Perfection of God.[9]

The Bahá'í analogy of the human heart as a mirror that often needs cleansing from the 'dust and dross' of the world can now be found in more recent publications on meditation, as well:

In relation to our practice of meditation, 'dust' could be seen in two ways. One is the immediate dust; the thoughts and feelings that are the consequences of whatever is happening for us today – an argument we have had, some good or bad news. The various meditation exercises, and skills we acquire from them, can help us to calm things down and clear our consciousness. The other is the more established dust; the ways of thinking and feeling that have become a habit for us, like having an anxious, over-active mind or a defeatist attitude. It is the regular effective practice that will layer by layer, polish this dust away. The more we practise polishing our 'mirror' with mindful, liberating, life-enhancing attitudes, the more they become part of us and the easier it is for us to receive and reflect the light.[10]

Also:

When we sit to meditate, we are turning away from the material world to the spiritual sun. We are performing meditation exercises that are polishing our mirror. And when we are practising regularly we are preventing dust resettling, polishing more stubborn dust and perfecting the finish of the mirror.[11]

So far, we have learned that living a life of virtues and practising meditation are among the primary tools for the purification of heart which leads to divine illumination. Another powerful means for cleansing the heart is invoking the name of God. Sacred texts of religious traditions support this notion:

> The name of the Lord is a strong tower; the righteous man runs into it and is safe.[12]

> Everything has its polish and the polish of hearts is *dhikrullah* [mention of God].[13]

> I beseech Thee, by Thy Name through which Thou turnest restlessness into tranquillity, fear into confidence, weakness into strength and abasement into glory . . .[14]

> It [the Greatest Name of God] should be fed upon by constant use in daily invocations, in trouble, under opposition . . . It is the name of comfort, protection . . .[15]

> Armed with the Power of Thy Name nothing can ever hurt me, and with Thy love in my heart all the world's afflictions can in no wise alarm me.[16]

> Call ye to mind the blessed Name of our peerless Beloved, the Abhá Beauty, in an uplifting spirit of unbounded ecstasy and delight, then unloose your tongues in His praise in such wise that the realm of the heart may be purged from the woes and sorrows of the world of water and clay . . .[17]

In the Bahá'í scriptures, in addition to 'dust' and 'dross', we may encounter other such terms as 'idle fancies', 'vain imaginings', and 'self and desire' that refer to the same obstacles which prevent our souls from reflecting the divine light:

> Burn ye away the veils with the fire of My love, and dispel

ye the mists of vain imaginings by the power of this Name through which We have subdued the entire creation.[18]

O My Servant! Thou art even as a finely tempered sword concealed in the darkness of its sheath and its value hidden from the artificer's knowledge. Wherefore come forth from the sheath of self and desire that thy worth may be made resplendent and manifest unto all the world.[19]

The Bahá'í Faith does not offer any particular form of meditation. Such matters seem to have been left to the individual believer, as we can see in the following passage:

There are no set forms of meditation prescribed in the teachings, no plan, as such, for inner development. The friends are urged – nay enjoined – to pray, and they also should meditate, but the manner of doing the latter is left entirely to the individual . . . [20]

Also:

Meditation is very important, and the Guardian [Shoghi Effendi] sees no reason why the friends should not be taught to meditate, but they should guard against superstitious or foolish ideas creeping into it.[21]

Bahá'ís think of meditation as quiet reflection, especially on passages of scripture.[22] Bahá'ís are taught that during meditation one can receive inspiration:

The inspiration received through meditation cannot be measured or quantified. God can inspire things into our minds that we had no previous knowledge of, if He desires to do so.[23]

Bahá'ís are not only encouraged to meditate but also to form gatherings for prayer and meditation:

The Guardian wishes me to assure you that he sees no objection to the friends coming together for meditation and prayer. Such a communion helps in fostering fellowship among the believers, and as such is highly commendable.[24]

However, prayer and meditation are generally considered private practices in the Bahá'í Writings. In addition, in the Bahá'í Faith, prayer and meditation should lead to the service of others. In fact, Bahá'u'lláh goes so far as defining a true human as one who dedicates his life to the service of his fellow man:

That one indeed is a man who, today, dedicateth himself to the service of the entire human race.[25]

4

THE SCIENTIFIC EVIDENCE

An enemy can hurt an enemy, and a man who hates can harm another man; but a man's own mind, if wrongly directed, can do him a far greater harm.

Dhammapada 3:42

In today's fast-paced world, most of us have to deal with the pressures of job, finances, family and relationships on a daily basis. These pressures can upset the natural rhythm of our body and its chemical balance. Over time, this can damage our immune system and make our bodies more susceptible to a variety of symptoms and diseases. These could range from minor nuisances such as headaches to more serious complications including stomach pain, heart problems, high blood pressure, or severe psychological disorders like anxiety, depression, anger, irritability and fear. A recent study reveals that today, between 60 to 90 per cent of visits to the doctor are for stress-related conditions.[1] This shows that most of us simply don't know how to prevent or fight stress. Going on a vacation, taking a long hot bath, getting a massage, working on our appearance, watching a relaxing TV show or a movie can certainly ease some of the stress, but they are not long-term solutions because they don't address the deeper roots of stress in our lives. Regular meditation does.

Consistent, daily engagement in the practice of meditation can be a great antidote to long-term stress because meditation goes straight to the source of the stress: our mind. Stress usually leads to a racing mind that leads us astray! We begin to think rapidly about things we have done in the past, are doing now, or might be doing in the future. By running from one negative scenario to another, we gradually exhaust our minds and our bodies. The most critical aspect of jumping from one negative thought to the next is that each is accompanied by certain emotional charge. For instance, feelings of worry, anxiety and fear may accompany our thoughts of future events; sorrow and guilt may colour our past memories; while anger and frustration may be associated with the things we are currently doing – and that's how most of the damage is done. Emotional responses triggered by racing thoughts tied to a sequence of imaginary, often illogical events can lead to incredible amounts of pressure.

In the field of meditation, these emotional responses are known as attachments. During meditation, we gradually learn to overcome emotional responses or attachments and become good at letting go of thoughts as clouds floating in the realm of our mind. Little by little, our stress level declines and we begin to enjoy a peaceful, focused and balanced mind. So, meditation enables us to manage stress at the deepest level – our mind. This does not mean that the causes of stress in the external world will disappear. Most of us will continue to face stressful situations. However, regular meditation will teach our mind to respond to 'stressors' in a more objective, less emotional manner. [2]

Relaxation Response

The mind is indeed restless . . . But by constant practice . . . the mind in truth can be trained. [3]

To fully appreciate how meditation can affect our health, we need to develop a proper understanding of the *fight-or-flight response* which is the basis of today's stress medicine. This physiological response is our body's natural, automatic and innate answer to a frightening or challenging situation. A sense of danger such as an imminent attack by a wild animal will stimulate the fight-or-flight response. Soon, chemicals such as adrenaline and stress hormones like cortisol are released into our bloodstream. The entire chemistry of our body including blood pressure, heart rate, and respiration quickly change, so that we can react to the imminent danger by either defending ourselves or running away from the source of the threat. Once the threat is removed, our mind and body return to their normal states.

The fight-or-flight response is indispensable to our physical survival. However, in today's stressful world, threats that trigger this mechanism are often psychological, not physical. [4] Most of us live in urban areas and rarely have to face a potential attack by a bear or a lion; yet hardly any of us escape for long from tensions sensed by a looming deadline, financial problems, family issues, bad relationships, loss of a loved one, and so forth. These tense situations release stress hormones such as cortisol into our bloodstream on a daily basis, even when our physical survival is not at stake. Over time, the build-up of such hormones causes stress-related illnesses. A powerful method for relieving our body from accumulated stress and returning it to its normal state is the *relaxation response*. Meditation and visualization techniques are among the best-known approaches for eliciting the relaxation response.

In his classic book *The Relaxation Response*, Dr Herbert Benson of Harvard Medical School, widely recognized as a pioneer in scientific studies of the healing impact of meditation, recommends four essential elements for eliciting the relaxation response. These elements are based on Benson's study of eastern and western meditation techniques:

1. *A peaceful place* for relaxation.

2. *A mental tool* to help the mind concentrate better, such as one's breath, a mantra or an object for gazing.

3. *A passive mindset* to be non-judgmental about our performance while engaged in meditation. So when intrusive thoughts enter the realm of the mind, we need to simply let them go, while gently bringing our attention back to the object of our concentration. Otherwise, the relaxation response will not take place. Dr Benson considers a passive

mindset as the most significant factor in evoking the relaxation response.

4. *A comfortable and relaxed posture*, with the exception of lying down which may lead to falling asleep.[5]

The relaxation response can change the chemistry of our body which will, in turn, help us to regain a healthy balance. The response triggers physiological changes such as a decrease in blood pressure, respiratory rate and heart rate, as well as an increase in the brain's alpha waves that signal a clear, calm, and relaxed mind.[6]

The Healing Power of Meditation

A father or a mother, or a relative, can indeed do good to a man; but his own right-directed mind can do to him a far greater good. [7]

One of the primary goals of meditation is to overcome the internal chatter, which will help quiet our conscious mind so that we can achieve a tranquil state. As the mind becomes steady, our central nervous system finds balance. This, in turn, leads to a relaxation of the rest of our physical systems, which allows the body to steadily repair and renew itself. [8] Therefore, the mind has the power to heal both physical and mental afflictions and bring us joy and peace.[9] So it is not remarkable that meditation and relaxation practices have over time found their way into mainstream medicine. Today, the physiological, psychological and spiritual benefits of these non-traditional approaches to healing are widely accepted. Gone are the days when, on a 1967 night Dr Benson, 'afraid of looking too flaky, waited until late at night to sneak 36 transcendental meditators into his lab to measure their heart rate, blood pressure, skin temperature and rectal temperature.' [10] Benson and others can now rely on decades of scientific research in the field.

Physiological Benefits of Meditation

Numerous studies have established the positive impact of meditation on a variety of physiological conditions. When done properly and consistently, meditation can take our body to a state more relaxed than even deep sleep, though we are fully awake and conscious inside.[11] This optimal condition gives our body a chance to start its self-healing process. Among all the physiological benefits of meditation, perhaps the one most frequently cited is the drop in blood pressure. Even the US National Institutes of Health (NIH) picks meditation as the most effective means of treating mild hypertension.[12] Their recommendation is based on a meta-analysis of 17 published studies from the medical literature in which a total of over 1,000 people with high blood pressure were treated using five different stress reduction techniques: simple biofeedback, relaxation-assisted biofeedback, progressive muscle relaxation, stress management training, and Transcendental Meditation (TM). The results showed that only TM resulted in significant clinical and statistical reductions in blood pressure. In addition, relaxation through meditation can lower blood cholesterol levels, mitigate the impact of arrhythmia (irregular heart beat), and help diabetic patients in decreasing the emotional reactions that mostly precede heart attacks.

Other studies show that medication can lessen the frequency of headaches and colds and can be effective in treating hypertension.[13] Newberg and Waldman report cases of meditation curing drug addictions and lessening the severity of psoriasis in patients.[14] Regular meditation also contributes to a decrease in symptoms or accelerates the healing process of many physical diseases such as stomach problems, allergies, muscle tension, arthritis, headaches, asthma, cancer, heart disease, skin problems, palpitations, and Temporomandibular Joint (TMJ).[15] After all, tension is a contributing factor to worsening the condition of all these diseases.

In a study of health insurance statistics, Dr Orme-Johnson found that meditators had 87 per cent fewer episodes of hospitalization for heart disease, 55 per cent fewer for benign and malignant tumours, and 30 per cent fewer for infectious diseases. On average, they also made over 50 per cent fewer visits to the doctor than did non-meditators.[16]

Meditation can also be effective in the treatment of insomnia. In one study, Dr Gregg Jacobs of Harvard Medical School found that 75 per cent of long-term insomniacs who were trained in relaxation, meditation and simple lifestyle changes learned to fall asleep within 20 minutes of going to bed.[17] Another study by Donald Miskiman, a researcher at the University of Alberta in Canada, showed that, through meditation, people with insomnia could fall asleep faster.[18] Similar results were obtained in a different study conducted at Rutgers University under the supervision of Robert Woolfolk.[19]

Additionally, studies by researchers at Harvard Medical School show that meditation can activate parts of the brain in charge of involuntary bodily functions such as digestion and blood pressure which are generally affected by stress. The Harvard researchers used functional magnetic resonance imaging (fMRI) to monitor the participants' brain activity during meditation. Results showed a significant role for meditation in treating stress-related physical conditions such as digestive problems, heart disease and infertility.[20] Finally, Blumenfeld found positive impacts for meditation in treating chronic pain as well as alcohol and drug addiction.[21]

Psychological Benefits of Meditation

Meditation and intensive prayer can also help us gain better control of our emotions. [22] When left unchecked, these emotions can often elevate our stress levels and cause a variety of psychological problems. Some of the more obvious mental benefits of meditation are a more relaxed mindset that leads to less anxiety and a reduction in the frequency and intensity of mood swings and anger episodes. It is not surprising that meditation practices which focus on mindfulness, such as mantra meditation and walking meditation, have proven useful in treating a wide range of psychological symptoms including anxiety, hypertension, depression and eating disorders.[23]

Life conditions and our responses to them can drive us to an internal chemical warfare[24] with ourselves. We often don't even realize this sort of warfare is going on inside us. When we don't deal with stress properly, our adrenal gland produces *cortisol*, a steroid hormone that increases blood sugar and suppresses our immune system. A weaker immune system means our bodies will have less resistance to illness and disease. On the other hand, if our response to stressful situations in life is positive and we engage in stress reduction or elimination practices such as prayer and meditation, our body will begin releasing *serotonin*, known as the *happiness hormone* – which incidentally is a misnomer because serotonin is a neurotransmitter, not a hormone. Serotonin greatly contributes to feeling happier, more confident, and in control of one's behaviour. Therefore, people with high levels of serotonin usually demonstrate more composure and are calmer under chaotic or stressful situations.

Prayer and meditation release helpful neurotransmitters such as dopamine and serotonin into our body and brain and help them function properly. This change in the neurochemistry of our brain also helps us attain a sense of joy, calm and safety and relieves symptoms of tension, sadness and anxiety. [25] Therefore, meditation can have a significantly positive influence over our mental and emotional well-being. It is a valuable tool in treating depression by increasing the availability of positive chemicals such as serotonin and tryptophan in our central nervous system, both of which play a critical role in mood elevation. In addition, persistent, regular and disciplined meditation can help us feel more confident and optimistic about life in general. Among other psychological benefits of meditation are fewer episodes of 'guilt feeling', and 'a decrease in unreasonable internal expectations, improved self-esteem, less intense grief reaction, and diminished separation anxiety'. [26] Meditation has also been applied with much success in the treatment of post-traumatic stress disorder. [27]

Spiritual Benefits of Meditation

Regular meditation also allows practitioners to develop a deeper level of spiritual relaxation that goes beyond stress reduction and the calming of the mind. It enables them to develop a greater appreciation for life in general, for themselves, and for others. It helps them nurture a deeper capacity for loving others and for being more compassionate and forgiving towards humans everywhere. This heightened level of self-awareness leads to a spiritual orientation in life that enables practitioners to feel detached from the mundane. Through reflection and contemplation on bigger questions in life such as *what's the meaning of life, why are we here, and where are we going*, they begin to see and appreciate the big picture. This helps them gain deeper insight into what matters most in life, which in turn enables them to find solutions to even the most complex and tragic problems that life throws at them such as a terminal disease, the loss of a loved one, or dealing with consequences of a natural disaster or a ravaging war:

> In her work with many cancer and AIDS patients, Dr Borysenko has observed that many are most interested in meditation as a way of becoming more attuned to the spiritual dimension of life. She reports that many die 'healed', in a state of compassionate self-awareness and self-acceptance.[28]

One of the first scientists to study the positive spiritual impacts of meditation was Dr Gregg Jacobs, a professor of psychiatry at Harvard Medical School and a colleague of Dr Herbert Benson in the pioneering research on the benefits of meditation. In one such study, Dr Jacobs compared the EEGs of a group of meditators to those of subjects who were asked to listen to books on tape. Over the next few months, the meditators produced far more Theta waves than the book listeners, which meant they were much more relaxed – the more Theta waves your brain produces, the more relaxed you are (see Figure 1).

Figure 1. Brainwaves

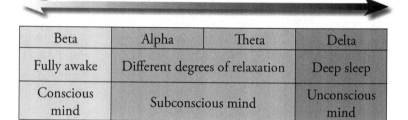

Beta	Alpha	Theta	Delta
Fully awake	Different degrees of relaxation		Deep sleep
Conscious mind	Subconscious mind		Unconscious mind

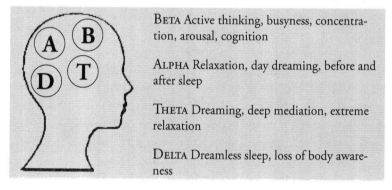

BETA Active thinking, busyness, concentration, arousal, cognition

ALPHA Relaxation, day dreaming, before and after sleep

THETA Dreaming, deep mediation, extreme relaxation

DELTA Dreamless sleep, loss of body awareness

Courtesy of Chris Brown: http://www.meditationdownloadproject.com/

Jacob's study showed that meditators were able to essentially deactivate the frontal areas of their brains that receive and process sensory information. They also lowered activity in the parietal lobe, a section of the brain near the top of the head that orients us in space and time. By shutting down the parietal lobe, meditators lost their sense of boundaries and felt more 'at one' with the universe.

Furthermore, scientific studies by Andrew Newberg and Mark Waldman – the authors of *How God Changes Your Brain* – also lend strong support to the idea that spiritual practices such as meditation can actually lead to neurochemical changes in our brains. In their studies, the authors observed brain functions of people of various faiths as they engaged in meditation. They concluded that such practices, even if they were not centred on the concept of a deity, increased the neural functioning of the brain and improved the emotional and physical well-being of the individual. Interestingly, they also learned that concentrated and long-term meditation and reflection on God can bring about permanent changes in the physical shape of parts of our brain that control our moods:

> One of the most unusual findings in our brain-scan studies involves the thalamus . . . The thalamus is the Grand Central Station of sensory processing: Every sensation, mood, and thought passes through it as the information is relayed to other parts of the brain . . . The thalamus plays a crucial role in identifying what is and isn't real, and it gives a sense of emotional meaning to the thoughts that emerge in the frontal lobe . . . the more you meditate on a specific object, be it God, or peace, the more active your thalamus becomes . . . if you exercise an idea over and over, your brain will begin to respond as though the idea was a real object in the world . . . The more you focus on God, the more God will be sensed as real . . . For advanced meditators . . . God, tranquility, and unity become an integral part of their lives, no longer a thought but a palpable experience.[29]

In addition, Newberg and Waldman learned that meditation can help us become more peaceful and compassionate towards others, while anger had negative consequences on brain activity:

> Anger interrupts the functioning of your frontal lobes. Not only do you lose the ability to be rational, you lose the awareness that you're acting in an irrational way. When your frontal lobes shut down, it's impossible to listen to the other person, let alone feel empathy or compassion. Instead, you are likely to feel self-justified and self-righteous, and when that happens, the communication process falls apart. Anger also releases a cascade of neurochemicals that actually destroy those parts of the brain that control emotional reactivity. It takes a lot of perseverance and training to respond to anger with kindness,

but this is exactly what spiritual teachers have been trying to teach for centuries. When you intensely and consistently focus on your spiritual values and goals, you increase the blood flow to your frontal lobes and anterior cingulate, which causes the activity in emotional centers of the brain to decrease. Conscious intention is the key, and the more you focus on your inner values, the more you can take charge of your life . . . meditation – be it religious or secular – enables you . . . to exercise your brain in loving and compassionate ways. [30]

Loving-kindness or compassion towards others (*metta*) has been high on the agenda of the Dalai Lama[31] for years. However, the leader of Tibet also has a keen interest in neuroscience as a potential pathway towards compassion towards all. After he watched brain surgery during a visit to an American medical school in the 1990s, the surgeon said to him that mental experiences – our thoughts, emotions, hopes, beliefs, and so on – were in fact products of chemical and electrical activity in the brain. The Dalai Lama then asked the surgeon if the reverse was possible. In other words, could our thoughts, emotions, feelings, or beliefs change the brain's activity, its circuitry, or its physical structure? The surgeon said no. To him, downward causation from a mental activity to the physical makeup of the brain was impossible. Yet the newly rediscovered concept of neuroplasticity[32] eventually proved the Dalai Lama right.

Neuroscientists have now documented how 'mere' thoughts can actually change the physical structure of the brain:

> Just thinking about playing a piano piece, over and over, can expand the region of motor cortex that controls those fingers; just thinking about depressive thoughts in new ways can dial down activity in one part of the brain that underlies depression and increase it in another, leading to clinical improvement.[33]

If that is the case, then it stands to reason that meditation, which involves concentration on certain thoughts or words, can also change the functioning or structure of the brain in an enduring way. This is the question that Professor Richard Davidson of the University of Wisconsin, Madison has tried to answer in collaboration with the Dalai Lama since 2000, some eight years after they initially met.

In 2007, after years of research, Davidson and his colleagues reported that meditation can indeed change attention capabilities in the human brain.[34] They also found that meditation increased production of gamma brainwaves,[35] which are tied to consciousness.[36] Recently, Davidson's team found that practising loving-kindness or compassion (*metta*) meditation can make long-lasting changes to certain parts of the brain and make us more empathetic:[37]

> In compassion meditation, as the French-born Buddhist monk Matthieu Ricard explained it to me when we were both visiting the Dalai Lama in Dharamsala for a meeting of neuroscientists and Buddhist scholars, you focus on the wish that all sentient beings be free of suffering. You generate an intense feeling of love for all beings, not fixating on individuals but encompassing all of humanity. It takes practice, since the natural tendency is to focus on one or a few specific suffering people.[38]

For his latest research, Davidson actually received support from the Dalai Lama himself who asked Buddhist scholars to volunteer their brains to Davidson's research. Davidson's colleague Antoine Lutz enlisted sixteen expert meditators for this particular study; nine Asian and seven European. These were monks with at least 10,000 hours of meditation practice. These are the monks we usually see wearing saffron robes. During the study, monks individually lay in a functional magnetic resonance imaging (fMRI) tube which detected the active and quiet regions of their brains during meditation. Lutz then compared the monks' readings to those of sixteen non-meditators of the same age group who simply underwent a crash course in compassion meditation. The non-meditators were members of the University of Wisconsin-Madison community.

> Each of the 32 subjects lay in the fMRI and turned compassion meditation on and off, on Lutz's command. Throughout, Lutz piped in happy sounds (a baby laughing and cooing), distressed ones (a woman who sounded as if she were in pain) and neutral ones (restaurant noise). Two regions lit up with activity.[39]

When the monks engaged in compassion meditation and heard the happy or distressed sounds, their *insulae* became noticeably active. The insula is a structure near the front of the brain that detects emotions, converts them into physiological responses such as elevated heart rate and blood pressure, and sends information about the changes to other parts of the brain to signal that a negative event has just affected us and that we should do something about it. In the case of the monks, insula activity was the greatest when they heard the distressed sounds. Also, the monks' insula activity was more pronounced than that of the novices.

But the study found something even more interesting in another area of the brain called the *temporal parietal juncture*, particularly the right hemisphere. Decade-long research by others had already confirmed that the temporal parietal juncture of the brain has the capability to perceive the mental and emotional state of others. For some examples, see studies by Decety and Chaminade,[40] Carr,[41] Saarela,[42] Immordino-Yang,[43] and Decety.[44]

Remarkably, Davidson and Lutz's research found that empathetic activity was significantly greater in the monks than the novices during periods when they were *not even meditating*. In other words, those thousands of hours of meditation by expert meditators had created *an enduring change* in the region of the brain that helps us show empathy and compassion towards others at all times. This finding essentially implies that we can train our brains to become more compassionate towards others through a systematic programme of meditation:

The Dalai Lama has long tried, through his teachings, to increase the world's supply of compassion and empathy. This study suggests that compassion meditation might do that, Davidson said in a statement: 'People are not just stuck at their respective set points' for compassion. 'We can take advantage of our brain's plasticity and train it to enhance these qualities.'[45]

Another follower of the Dalai Lama who agreed to participate in meditation research was meditation expert monk Mingyur Rinpoche, who had been drawn to a life of contemplation at the age of sixteen. Rinpoche had also been a subject in some of the early studies of advanced meditators that Richard Davidson conducted at the University of Wisconsin.[46]

In a 2009 study, Rinpoche was put in an fMRI machine at the Waisman Laboratory for Brain Imaging and Behavior at the University of Wisconsin-Madison. They secured his head to make sure it didn't move during the procedure and then asked him to meditate in three different ways:

- remain open and present, to rest in the nature of mind
- meditate on loving-kindness and compassion
- practice *shamatha* or focusing on a single object during meditation[47]

Rinpoche later described his experience:

> When they tested me, I had to meditate for about two minutes and then stop. Meanwhile, the scientists were in another room, having fun and drinking coffee. Sometimes they would say loudly: 'Compassion, please.' Then, two minutes later, 'Stop compassion!' Then, 'Please meditate on compassion again.' And, 'Stop meditating on compassion!' And then: 'Focus!' 'No focus!' 'Focus!' 'No focus!' And then: 'Be present!' 'Don't be present!' It was quite difficult. They did this over and over.[48]

The test results baffled the scientists. The gamma waves from Rinpoche's brain activity were so high and out of the ordinary that the scientists thought that the machine was broken. However, they noticed that when Rinpoche was asked to stop meditating, his gamma waves went down to normal levels. They replicated the results with several other expert meditators:

> Yes, at first they thought there was something wrong with the machine, because the gamma waves, the frequency of electrical signals occurring in the brain when many neurons work together, increased a great deal, as did the activity in the left side of the brain. Normally, when the level of gamma waves gets to a certain point, you are totally crazy, out of control.[49]

There was, of course, nothing wrong with Rinpoche. Thousands of hours of concentration and meditation had enabled him to master self-control to the point of generating extraordinary gamma waves in his brain activity.

> Scientists have told me that there are many neurons in the brain, and that these neurons are able to make new connections with each other. The stronger the connection becomes, the more powerful the message will be. That's why, if you panic, at first it may be small, but if you always think about it, then the connections become bigger and bigger, and the panic stronger and stronger.[50]

Conclusion

Scientific research in the field of meditation is now over half a century old. A substantial body of knowledge which started accumulating from daring experiments in the labs of pioneers like Herbert Benson and Gregg Jacobs at Harvard Medical School gathered more momentum as years went by. Over subsequent decades, many academicians including Daniel Goleman of Harvard, Jon Kabat-Zinn of the University of Massachusetts, Andrew Newberg of the University of Pennsylvania and Mark Waldman of Loyola Marymount, Zoran Josipovic of New York

University, and Richard Davidson of the University of Wisconsin, as well as countless experts in the field of neuroscience, have added to the rich history of investigating the physiological, psychological and spiritual benefits of meditation.

Today, the positive impact of meditation on human health is well-established. Meditation is now widely recognized as one of the best ways to relax the mind, help gain control over thoughts, feelings and behaviour, improve general health, and even create lasting change in the structure and functionality of the brain.

Yet we must remember that the healing of the mind, body and soul through meditative practices is a gradual process. It can be compared to the slow movement of a great river whose water slowly but surely makes its way to the sea. The movement of the water may not be easily observable from afar, but it is happening. If we walk closer to the river, we will see the water flowing. So, when you commit to become a regular meditator, watch for the slightest progress you make and give yourself credit every step of the way. Pay close attention to any positive changes in your way of thinking, feeling and acting that have come about as a result of your newly found love. If you see progress, be kind and compassionate to yourself. Take time to celebrate, no matter how small the progress might be.[51]

5
GETTING READY TO MEDITATE[1]

The mind is wavering and restless, difficult to guard and restrain; let the wise man straighten his mind as a maker of arrows makes his arrows straight.

Dhammapada 3:33

Anyone who is interested can be trained to meditate. However, meditation involves long-term commitment, unwavering determination and persistent striving. As we read in the previous chapter, the benefits of meditation are many; however, those of us who choose to embark on this journey need to bear in mind that we cannot be impatient with ourselves or with the process. We also need to look for a meditation method that appeals to us.[2] Gradually, as our meditation practice deepens, we may want to include other types of meditation that resonate with us in our daily practice.

Making time to meditate daily should be viewed as making time to come home to our deeper self. It is a time for attaining inner peace and renewing ourselves. As we gain experience, we will come to realize that our thoughts are simply thoughts.[3] They are neither us nor have a reality of their own. This is a very liberating feeling which will empower us to avoid feeling tense, nervous or forced to act in a certain manner merely because a thought entered our mind. For example, if a thought came to mind that we needed to do certain things in the course of a day, we can step back from the thought and examine it more clearly. We can then prioritize the things that need to be done and make the proper decisions about them. We will also be able to stop when we really need to.

With persistence, you will gradually notice that meditation will not only help you but those around you. Slowly but surely, communicating with others will become easier. Family, friends and colleagues will find your company more enjoyable. When they see the change in you, they may get inspired to try meditation themselves. Our thoughts and our actions affect the world around us. If we want to have peace in the world, we should start one mind at a time – our own.[4]

The effects of meditation are cumulative. Changes in thought patterns and behaviours don't usually happen overnight. The more time we spend training and disciplining our minds with meditation, the more pronounced the impact on our mental and physical well-being. This alone should provide plenty of motivation for us to engage in regular, daily meditation. Even in very busy days, we must do our utmost to find at least a few minutes to meditate. To make a lasting difference, meditation must become a 'top priority' in our lives.[5] Practising meditation in short bursts once or twice a day is a good start, but it is not enough. The practice must eventually lead to being mindful while engaging in any casual activity – walking, standing, sitting, lying down, working, taking baths, eating and drinking, talking to others, and doing chores around the house. The ultimate goal is to make meditation second nature.

A Typical Meditation Session

Before engaging in meditation, wear loose, comfortable clothing. Avoid wearing glasses, tight belts, watch bands, shoes or anything that might put pressure on your body. Have a blanket handy, too. Meditation can slow down your metabolism and drop your body's temperature.[6] The meditation area can be indoors or outdoors in the middle of nature. However, it is best if the area is quiet, the temperature is moderate and your body is not exposed to direct sunlight.

When you begin your first meditation session, you will soon realize that your mind is quite busy and distracted. Various thoughts run endlessly through your head. These range from remembering previous conversations to making a shopping list and so forth. Remember, this is completely normal. In fact, this is how most of us are conditioned to operate. Our brains have learned to go from one thought to another during our waking hours. The early stages in meditation are among the most critical because most of us tend to get frustrated early on in the process. We expect early success, and often we either don't get it or we come upon it in small doses. Thus, it is absolutely critical not to give up. Imagine yourself climbing a mountain. It is hard, but you have the satisfaction of knowing that once you get to the top, an incredible vista is waiting for you.

With perseverance and training, your mind will gradually become calmer and less domineering. Sooner than you might imagine, you will begin to reap the rewards. Another essential thing to remember in the early stages of meditation is to avoid the tendency to criticize yourself for not being fully in charge of your mind. Again, bear in mind that at this point in the training, you are simply *practising* meditation. In other words, you are a novice – not a master[7] – so don't expect a miracle from your mind. Instead of being judgemental with yourself or trying to flawlessly manage your thoughts, be forgiving and compassionate towards yourself. Accept whatever progress you are making during your first session. As thoughts enter your mind, simply let them leave, just as clouds drift away, one after the other without attachment or emotion. Apply the same principle and attitude to all unwanted thoughts during the day. As they come to you, let them leave. If you don't immediately succeed, give yourself more time. Remember to be patient and forgiving to yourself. You can also think of your mind as a small child, whose grandparent has taken her out for a walk on a narrow path in nature. The child is full of zest and energy and thus runs from one side of the path to the other. At one point, she chases a butterfly; at another she picks a wild flower. Every time we become conscious of the child – which in this analogy is our mind straying from the road – we must bring her back to the path gently and in a sweet and caring manner, just as a loving grandparent would. Remember: don't get frustrated with yourself, regardless of the number of times you need to bring your mind back to the object of your meditation.

One of the great advantages of meditation is that its beneficial effects do not diminish with the passage of time, but rather become potent for those who take meditation seriously. The calming effects of meditation are not limited to the duration of the meditation session. They persist throughout the day. We maintain some of the calm that we experienced during our meditation and can recreate some of that peace over the course of our day. Through meditation, we gradually learn to modify our reactions to daily life situations. We can remember the serenity we experienced during our last meditation session and look forward to our next one. This way, meditation can become like an oasis we can go to during chaotic times in our life.[8]

Finally, do we need to have a meditation teacher such as an Indian guru or a Buddhist monk to teach us how to meditate? Not necessarily:

When meditation is associated with one Indian guru, one Tibetan tulku, and you find out that he has been sleeping with his students' wives, your whole belief in the process can be shattered. If you are in one of the many cultlike meditation groups around that are inflated with a sense of their own specialness and you utter the wrong thought, you may be rejected. The world is full of people wanting to steal your inner authority. But meditating on your own, in the context of your daily life, and using your senses and your life as your feedback mechanism is a great way to go.[9]

How Often Should We Meditate?

The mind is indeed restless . . . It is indeed hard to train. But by constant practice . . . the mind in truth can be trained.[10]

Effective meditation requires daily practice even if it is only for a few minutes. Start off with five minutes the first week and add another five minutes until you build up your sessions to 20 minutes once or twice daily.[11] When you are ready, gradually increase your sessions to 30 minutes or longer. Do not force yourself to go through multiple sessions or periods of time longer than you are comfortable with. The length and frequency should come naturally and only as a result of the joy and peace you find in the practice of meditation.[12]

For most people, the ideal range to change the neural functioning of the brain through meditation is between 20–40 minutes of daily practice. There is a correlation between the length of time we spend on meditation and the impact it leaves on our brain.[13] The longer and more frequently we meditate, the quicker and more lasting the changes that occur in our brain. This is why we shouldn't expect noticeable change after just a couple of sessions.

During meditation sessions, use a gentle alarm clock so you don't have to stop every few minutes to check the time. It is essential that you give your undivided attention to the meditation practice. The best time to meditate is early morning when you are most alert. The other option is late evening, provided that you do not feel sleepy when you start your session.[14]

Silence as a Spiritual Discipline

Be still and know that I am God.[15]

Using silence as a spiritual practice has a long history in religion. It is a central element of meditation in both eastern and western traditions. The famous 14th-century mystic Meister Eckhart said:

Nothing in all creation is so like God as silence.[16]

St Bernard of Clairvaux is believed to have said:

Continual silence, and removal from the noise of the things of this world and forgetfulness of them, lifts up the heart and asks us to think of the things of heaven and sets our heart upon them.[17]

And St Diodorus is credited with the following statement: 'Silence is the mother of holy and lofty thoughts.'[18]

Silence is an indispensable part of training our mind and a great aid in our spiritual discipline. In his book *The Way to God*, Gandhi writes:

> Before modern civilization came upon us, at least six to eight hours of silence out of twenty-four were vouchsafed to us. Modern civilization has taught us to convert night into day and golden silence into brazen din and noise. What a great thing it would be if we in our busy lives, could retire into ourselves each day, for at least a couple of hours, and prepare our minds to listen to the voice of the great silence. The divine radio is always singing if we could only make ourselves ready to listen to it, but it is impossible to listen without silence.[19]

Ram Dass agrees with Gandhi:

> I recall that as a Harvard professor I had FM in my car and stereo in my office and home; I was constantly surrounded by music – even with a speaker in my bathroom. In addition, there were paintings on all the walls and decorations in my car. Slowly, as meditation changed my perception of the universe, I started to crave simplicity. I placed objects on the walls that reminded me of higher possibilities . . . I found that I was beginning to appreciate the silence and was content to enjoy a few pieces of music or art thoroughly rather than fill every space with sound and with imagery. At times, I even felt the total contentment that comes from sitting in silence in a purely white room.[20]

Silence as a spiritual practice as well as an approach to self-discipline finds support in various religions:

> When a man knows the solitude of silence, and feels the joy of quietness, he is then free from fear and sin and he feels the joy of the Dhamma.[21]

39

Blessed is he who, at the hour of dawn, centring his thoughts on God, occupied with His remembrance, and supplicating His forgiveness, directeth his steps to the Mashriqu'l-Adhkár and, entering therein, seateth himself in silence to listen to the verses of God, the Sovereign, the Mighty, the All-Praised.[22]

... there is a sign (from God) in every phenomenon: the sign of the intellect is contemplation and the sign of contemplation is silence, because it is impossible for a man to do two things at one time – he cannot both speak and meditate.[23]

PART II

MEDITATION TECHNIQUES

Those who make channels for water control the waters; makers of arrows make the arrows straight; carpenters control their timber; and the wise control their own minds.

Dhammapada 6: 80

Our mind usually functions as though it is on automatic pilot.[1] We have a tendency to be not totally conscious of the things we are doing. A good example is when we are driving a car. We drive from point A to point B without much awareness of the things we see along the way. Even if we try to focus on the driving, we find that it is not easy to keep our mind occupied with that task for any length of time. It almost feels like our mind has a mind of its own! Our thoughts can become especially overwhelming when we face trials and tests in life, thus clouding our perception of the present. Through various meditation techniques, we can learn to gain mastery over our minds and lead a peaceful, happy and productive life. Let us now turn to some of the most well-known approaches to meditation.

6

SINGLE OBJECT MEDITATION

Be still, and know that I am God.

Psalms 46:10

Meditation on a single object is one of the most popular methods of meditation. It is easy and enjoyable and can lead to concentration, enhanced memory skills and focused concentration of the mind. This technique requires the use of a single object such as a picture, a candle, a pebble, a shell, a flower or a leaf. Place the object of meditation at enough distance from you to see its details without straining the eyes. Set the object at a height that allows you to look straight ahead. You can darken the room if the background is distracting. Sit comfortably in a chair or on the floor with your back straight, your hands resting either on your sides or on your lap. The palms could face up or down, as you desire. Take a few deep breaths to quiet your mind. Then relax and breathe easily and normally. Begin your practice by quietly focusing on the object with open eyes. Treat the object as if you have never seen one like it before – that is, with much interest and curiosity, exploring its various parts. Pay attention to its colour, shape, and texture.

For instance, if you are gazing at a flower, direct your attention at only one spot or let your eyes examine the whole flower, i.e. the stem, the leaves, the petals and the centre. Focus on the colours, the shapes – the rounded areas as well as the edges, the texture – the smooth and rough areas. During this meditation, make sure you are not straining and there is no tension in your eyelids. So the practice needs to be done calmly, slowly and enjoyably.

Next, close your eyes and, in a relaxed manner, try to see the object in your mind. You may have to repeat this process a few times before you can see the image clearly in your mind's eye.[1]

Remember, if your mind wanders, gently bring it back to your object of meditation. The guiding principle in this and all other meditation practices is to be kind and gentle to yourself and avoid criticizing and judging your ability. You can start your practice for five minutes daily and gradually increase it to 20 minutes.

Candle-gazing Meditation Practice

One approach to single object meditation is candle-gazing meditation. Place a lighted candle at a distance which allows you to see the details of the flame without straining. Take a few breaths to calm your mind. Begin to gaze at the candle flame for a few minutes. Then close your eyes and try to see the candle flame in your mind. Repeat this process again by gazing at the candle, followed by recreating the image of the candle flame in your mind. When unwelcome thoughts arise, let them fly away like birds across the sky of your mind. Breathe naturally in and out as you do this meditation.

7

ANAPANASATI ('BREATH AWARENESS') AND VIPASSANA ('INSIGHT') *MEDITATION*

By arising in faith and watchfulness, by self-possession and self-harmony, the wise man makes an island for his soul which many waters cannot overflow.

Dhammapada 2:25

Anapanasati and Vipassana are ancient Buddhist meditation techniques that date back to the time of Buddha. It is believed that these techniques were used by the Buddha himself to attain enlightenment. For many centuries, Buddhists of different traditions have used these two techniques together as a primary approach to meditation. Through concentration on the *in* and *out* flow of breath, Anapanasati calms the meditator's mind, while in Vipassana, the focus on the breath alone is released to concentration on whatever arises. In practice, Anapanasati gives rise to Vipassana.[1]

In the Satipatthana Sutta, the Buddha is believed to have said the following about Anapanasati:

Breathing in long, he discerns that he is breathing in long; or breathing out long, he discerns that he is breathing out long. Or breathing in short, he discerns that he is breathing in short; or breathing out short, he discerns that he is breathing out short . . . Always mindful, he breathes in; mindful he breathes out.[2]

45

To do the Vipassana meditation, start off by taking three deep breaths. Then, let your breathing take on its own natural rhythm. To do the breath awareness (Anapanasati) part, either concentrate on the air that is flowing in and out of your nostrils or simply observe the rise and fall of your abdomen. Give full attention to each in-breath, out-breath, and the pause between the two. When your mind wanders, ever so gently bring it back to the breath.[3]

Larry Rosenberg, the author of *Breath by Breath,* has an effective technique for dealing with distractions. He encourages the meditator to move from a *doggy mind* to a *lion mind*:

One time when I was visiting a friend, he kept playing with his dog, throwing a plastic bone for the dog to go fetch. It not only wasn't a real bone, it wasn't even a convincing fake; pieces of meat were painted on the plastic. Yet no matter how many times he threw the bone, the dog ran after it, with great excitement. He kept chasing this plastic bone, which had no nourishment whatsoever, as if it could somehow satisfy him. Suddenly I realized: that's my mind, chasing after thoughts. The mind doesn't think it's chasing a plastic bone with pieces of meat painted on it, of course. It thinks it's pursuing something that will have a vital effect on its life. But if we look more closely at the objects that the mind chases, we notice a similar lack of nourishment. In contrast to that, think of a lion. Can you imagine how a lion – sitting in that majestic way they have – would react if you threw him a bone (especially a plastic one)? He wouldn't even notice. He'd just stare at you. Lions stay focused on the source. That's the attitude we need to have, sitting with that deep calm, that steadiness of purpose, not chasing after every bone that flies our way. We need to develop lion mind . . . our practice is to try to go from doggy mind to something more like lion mind, in which there is a deep steadiness.[4]

As your mind gradually begins to quiet down, move on to the second phase of your practice. In this phase, you no longer need your breath as the only object of concentration. Instead, use the breath simply as an anchor. Sit down, breathe and observe whatever happens. Don't hold on to your thoughts and emotions as they come and go. Don't try to push them away, either. Rosenberg describes Vipasana as the practice of 'clear seeing', and offers this insight into the nature and the outcome of this meditation method:

Just relax, breathe in, and know what's there. Whatever is in you starts to present itself. This way of attending to your experience, watching its nature from moment to moment, from breath to breath, takes us to another dimension of consciousness, one which is spacious and silent. The silent mind is tremendously fulfilling.[5]

8

MINDFULNESS OF THE PRESENT MOMENT

A third mindful meditation technique is mindfulness of the present moment. This approach is based on the notion that *real life is the life of the present. The rest is only an illusion.* Confucius said:

> Everything has beauty, but not everyone sees it.[1]

The human mind has a tendency to consistently put the attention either on the past or on the future. In his classic book *How to Stop Worrying and Start Living*, Dale Carnegie gives an interesting example of how we tend to dedicate precious moments of our present dreaming about an unknown future:

> One of the most tragic things I know about human nature is that all of us tend to put off living. We are dreaming of some magical rose garden over the horizon – instead of enjoying the roses that are blooming outside our windows.[2]

Carnegie reinforces this point by quoting the writer and humourist Stephen Leacock:

> How strange it is our little procession of life! The child says, 'when I am a big boy.' But what is that? The big boy says, 'When I grow up.' And then, grown up, he says, 'When I get married.' But what is that after all? The thought changes to

'When I'm able to retire.' And then, when retirement comes, he looks back over the landscape traversed; a cold wind seems to sweep over it, somehow he has missed it all, and it is gone. Life, we learn too late, is in the living, in the tissue of every day and hour.[3]

In reality, the most valuable possession we have is today. By being totally absorbed in what we are doing at any given moment of our lives, mindfulness can help train our minds to avoid dwelling on the dead yesterdays and unborn tomorrows.

To practise mindfulness we need to focus on the task at hand, whether it is working at the office or doing household chores. When your thoughts wander, attaching themselves to the regrets of the past or getting stuck in the fear and worry of the future, let your ego know that you will not let such thoughts ruin the gift of the precious present moment any more. Allow such thoughts to move on like clouds in the sky without attaching yourself to them or the emotions they have hidden behind them.[4]

If your mind wanders, don't get angry or quit. Instead, say 'Whoa!' Using this simple expression can be a fun wake-up call to tame your mind back to the task at hand – the practice of mindfulness.[5]

We can think of mindfulness as a state of consciousness that is characterized by bringing our attention to our present experience with a sense of **open curiosity**. When we practise mindfulness, chores become enjoyable if we can bring our attention to the experience of doing them. Consequently, what now seems routine and mundane can become a 'precious experience'.

Here is what the Buddha said about mindfulness:

And further, monks, a monk, in going forward and back, applies clear comprehension; in looking straight on and looking away, he applies clear comprehension; in bending and in stretching, he applies clear comprehension; in wearing robes and carrying the bowl, he applies clear comprehension; in eating, drinking, chewing and savoring, he applies clear comprehension; in walking, in standing, in sitting, in falling asleep, in waking, in speaking and in keeping silence, he applies clear comprehension. Thus he lives contemplating the body in the body . . . [6]

In the above passage, Buddha is essentially recommending mindfulness as a living meditation. It does not require escaping to a secluded place. You can practise this approach anywhere, regardless of the things that go on around you.[7] The beauty of the practice of mindfulness as an adjunct practice to our daily meditation is clearly illustrated in the following passage:

There is magic in the sun shining, the rain falling, the plants growing. There is magic in our feet on the earth, in the wind on our faces, in a beautiful sunset, in a bird soaring. This is the beauty of ordinary things that permeates our world, but that we rarely appreciate unless we go beyond the rational and logical mind. In the simplicity and stillness of meditation arises an awareness of these subtler and more illusory qualities. The magic is all around us, in everything, unassuming, undemanding, just being ordinary. It is the worry, confusions and anxieties that are extra-ordinary. When we let go of the 'extra', we sink into the 'ordinary' beauty of things as they are. This is seen in a Japanese haiku poem that reads:

> Among the grasses
> An unknown flower
> Blooming white.[8]

To show the significance of mindfulness, Zen Buddhists have a story of the Buddha and a flower. They say that one day the Buddha held up a flower in front of a large group of monks and nuns. The audience was thinking very hard to figure out the meaning behind the Buddha's gesture. Then, suddenly, the Buddha smiled because a monk by the name of Mahakashyapa smiled at him and the flower he was holding. This monk was the only person who smiled and as the Buddha was smiling back at him, he said that he had a treasure of insight, and that he had transmitted it to Mahakashyapa. If we keep thinking when someone shows us a flower, we miss the flower. That applies to everything that goes on around us in our lives.[9]

Every activity during the day can also potentially provide an opportunity to fully appreciate life and strengthen your mindfulness. What follows are some techniques for living in the present moment.

Samu (Mindful Chore)

Samu is usually regarded as a form of meditation in Zen Buddhism and is performed during manual labour. It is a vital part of the meditational life of Zen monks. In Zen monasteries, many hours are devoted each day to chores such as dusting, sweeping, polishing the floors, cleaning the toilets, weeding and gardening, and paying close attention to each chore as it is being done. This practice provides meditators with a great opportunity to quiet the chatter of their minds. This practice is not just for Zen monks. You can use the same approach to train your mind and arrive at peace.[10]

When doing daily chores, try to remember to do only one thing at a time. When your mind begins to wander, *gently* bring it back to the task at hand. For instance, when doing the dishes, you may be thinking about drinking your tea afterwards, and thus try to wash the dishes as fast as possible so that you can sit down and drink your tea. But when you live your life mindfully, doing the dishes will be the task you will concentrate on until it is finished.

Mindful Eating

You can begin mindful eating by smiling to yourself and becoming aware of 'seeing' the food you are about to eat. Pay close attention to its shape, colour and scent. Note the anticipation in your mind of the food you are about to eat. The next step is to reach for food mindfully. Raise your arm and lift the food into your mouth. As you put the food into your mouth, be mindful of the touch of the food on your tongue and how it tastes in your mouth as you are chewing it. Then, be mindful of the act of swallowing.[11]

Eat slowly and mindfully, taking the time to enjoy every bite. Chew at least twenty times before you swallow. During mindful eating meditation, when other thoughts come to your mind, *gently* bring your mind back to the food. Throughout your practice, continue to be mindful of seeing, smelling, reaching, touching, tasting, chewing, swallowing and enjoying.

Mindful Shower

When you shower, *know* that you are taking a shower. Pay attention to the scent of the soap and every part of your body as you wash it. Be mindful of the running water. Note its temperature as it cascades over your skin. The litmus test for mindful bathing is this: by the time your bath is over, your mind should feel as peaceful and relaxed as your body!

Mindful Communication

One of the major causes of family tension is poor communication skills. If you want to live a mindful life and enjoy the peace and serenity it brings you, pay attention to the words you utter and observe silence[12] when needed. What you communicate to others should be clear, considerate and compassionate.

When communicating, open your body in a relaxed and good posture while standing. Imagine a string at the crown of your head is comfortably pulling you up and properly aligning your spine. This practice not only reduces fatigue but will also help you be more open to the other people you communicate with.[13]

During conversations, look at others with warm and smiling eyes. By so doing, the act of looking becomes a prayer and a meditation by itself.[14]

Here are more suggestions for mindful communication:

- Pay close attention to what the other person is communicating.
- As you listen, bring yourself to the present moment by taking some mindful breaths now and then.
- Notice how the tendency to come up with an answer, to agree or disagree, can take your attention away from what the other person is trying to say.
- Just let go of the mental chatter and listen wholeheartedly. When it is time for you to respond, give careful attention to your own words, addressing what the other person has communicated to you. Allow your words to come from deep within you.[15]

A Day of Mindfulness

In his book The *Miracle of Mindfulness*, Nhat Hanh suggests that, ideally, we should practise mindfulness all day long, every day. But since this is difficult to accomplish, we should devote at least an entire day out of the week to the practice of mindfulness, perhaps Saturdays.

Pick a day that works best for you. When you wake up that morning, remind yourself that today is the day of mindfulness. Once you leave bed, wash your hands and face, brush your teeth and go through all other morning routines in a calm way with total mindfulness. When your thoughts scatter, *gently* bring them back to what you are doing with a smile on your face. Your morning bath, for instance, should be done slowly and mindfully so that by the time you are done you feel quite refreshed.

In the course of the day of mindfulness, do every task slowly and mindfully, whether it is brushing your teeth, drinking your tea, or doing household chores, Avoid the tendency to carry out a task to simply get it over with. Even your conversations need to be conducted mindfully as you pay close attention to the words you hear and the ones you are about to say. With enough practice, the day of mindfulness can begin to penetrate your other days of the week, enabling you to ultimately live your entire week in mindfulness.[16]

Alternatively, you can select a particular activity – such as opening a door, answering a telephone call, brushing your teeth, or going on the Internet – and make it your mindful activity for the day, week or month. In doing this, seemingly unimportant daily routines can become tools for the development of a calm attitude as a way of life.

To begin, choose a specific activity such as driving your car, maybe for an entire day. with as much attention as you possibly can. During the 'mindful driving day', instead of getting in your car and heading towards your destination as you listen to the radio, leave a few minutes earlier than usual so you have more time to practise your mindful driving. Sit behind the steering wheel and take a few deep breaths to calm your mind and body. Then, remind yourself that you are doing the mindful driving to help you develop a more peaceful mind. Proceed to drive calmly and attentively as you enjoy the surrounding nature. With this technique, the routine task of driving can become a safe, pleasant and peaceful experience.[17]

In addition to choosing specific tasks as a means of practising mindfulness, we can also use interruptions as wake-up calls. We usually react to interruptions which we consider 'distractions' with annoyance. Yet such distractions can become positive experiences which can even lead to a calmer mind, if we change our perception of them by allowing them to become tools in our practice of mindfulness. So next time the telephone rings or someone asks you for your opinion while you are engaged in another task, use that as an opportunity to practise mindfulness of the present moment.[18]

Cultivating Generosity Through Mindfulness

One approach to cultivating the virtue of generosity through the practice of mindfulness is the use of a 'mindfulness jar'. To do this practice, we need to have an empty jar or vase and a container for our loose change. Every time we are mindful of the things we do – mindful communication, mindful eating, mindful driving, mindful house chores, and so forth – we drop a coin in the mindfulness jar. We can decide how much we want to put in the jar based on the actions we do mindfully. A few times per year, we can empty the jar and donate the money to the charity of our choice. This way, we not only become motivated to practise mindfulness with the intention of having a more peaceful mind, soul and body – but we can also cultivate the God-given seed of generosity that is within our innermost self.

9

MINDFULNESS OF GOD: PRACTISING THE PRESENCE OF GOD

> I keep the Lord always before me: because he is at my right
> hand, I shall not be moved. Therefore my heart is glad, and my
> soul rejoices: my body also dwells secure.
>
> *Psalms 16:8–9*

Another approach to mindfulness is the practice of visualizing God's presence, or God-consciousness, in our daily life as a
constant companion. The sacred literature of different religious
traditions suggest that being mindful of God leads to a sense of
spiritual joy and serenity and is conducive to God's protection and
good-pleasure:

> O Thou . . . Whose presence is the hope of such as are wholly
> devoted to Thy will . . . Whose countenance is the companion
> of those who have recognized Thy truth . . . [1]

> Thy presence is the ardent desire of such as yearn to behold
> Thy face. [2]

> . . . in thy presence there is fullness of joy. [3]

> . . . be of them whose minds are firmly fixed and grounded in
> God. [4]

. . . remain conscious of God, so that you might attain to a happy state.[5]

. . . the garment of God-consciousness is the best of all.[6]

Verily, the noblest of you in the sight of God is the one who is most deeply conscious of Him. Behold, God is all-knowing, all-aware.[7]

. . . man can find peace in the peace of his God.[8]

Think of me therefore at all times; remember thou me and fight. And with mind and reason on me, thou shalt in truth come to me.[9]

For if a man thinks of the Spirit Supreme with a mind that wanders not . . . he goes to that Spirit of Light.[10]

Oh, verily, they who are close to God – no fear need they have, and neither shall they grieve; they who have attained to faith and have always been conscious of Him. For them there is the glad tidings [of happiness] in the life of this world and in the life to come; [and since] nothing could ever alter [the outcome] of God's promises, this, this is the triumph supreme![11]

He [the Prophet Muhammad] said: It [*ihsan*] is to worship Allah [God] as though you are seeing Him, and while you see Him not yet truly He sees you.[12]

[The Prophet Muhammad said] Be mindful of Allah, and Allah will protect you. Be mindful of Allah, and you will find Him in front of you. If you ask, ask of Allah; if you seek help, seek help of Allah.[13]

Be mindful of Allah, you will find Him before you. Get to

know Allah in prosperity and He will know you in adversity. Know that what has passed you by was not going to befall you and that what has befallen you was not going to pass you by. And know that victory comes with patience, relief with affliction, and ease with hardship.[14]

. . . it behoveth the people of truth that...they should walk upon the earth as though they were in the presence of God . . . Such must be their state that their eyes should behold the evidences of His might, their tongues and hearts make mention of His name, their feet be set towards the lands of His nearness, and their hands take fast hold upon His precepts.[15]

The practice of the presence of God finds support in the life of the Báb, as seen in the following story told by 'Abdu'l-Bahá advising the Bahá'ís to always be mindful of God in their daily activities:

His Holiness the Báb said, 'I worked in a commercial store at an early age. Whenever I had to write the address on a bale or read an address therefrom, I would lower my head and bow before God. In this way, I had God in my mind, even in this small task. My goal was God and under all conditions He was in my view.'[16]

Another great resource for living a God-centred life is a small book titled *The Practice of the Presence of God* which contains words of Brother Lawrence, who lived in the 17th century CE. This small book, compiled after Brother Lawrence's death, is a treasure-trove of practical advice for practising God's presence in our daily lives. The language of the book is simple, inspiring and engaging. The book's main theme is to encourage us to live a life of 'continual conversation' with God:

That we might accustom ourselves to a continual conversation with Him, with freedom and in simplicity. That we need only to recognize God intimately present with us, to address ourselves to Him every moment, that we may beg His assistance for knowing His will in things doubtful, and for rightly performing those which we plainly see He requires of us, offering them to Him before we do them, and giving Him thanks when we have done. That in this conversation with God we are also employed in praising, adoring, and loving Him incessantly, for His infinite goodness and perfection.[17]

Brother Lawrence teaches that our goal in life should be to become 'the most perfect worshipers of God we can possibly be'.[18] To him, God was the end of all of his 'thoughts and desires' and everything he did was for His love:

> That when he [Brother Lawrence] began his business, he said to God, with a filial trust in Him: O my God, since Thou art with me, and I must now, in obedience to Thy commands, apply my mind to these outward things, I beseech Thee to grant me the grace to continue in Thy presence; and to this end do Thou prosper me with Thy assistance, receive all my works, and possess all my affections. As he proceeded in his work he continued his familiar conversation with his Maker, imploring His grace, and offering to Him all his actions.[19]

The practice of the presence of God came naturally to Brother Lawrence. In his letters, he recommended this approach to others:

> I should communicate to you the method by which I arrived at that habitual sense of God's presence . . . I renounced, for the love of Him, everything that was not He, and I began to live as if there was none but He and I in the world . . . I beheld Him in my heart as my Father, as my God. I worshiped Him the oftenest that I could, keeping my mind in His holy presence, and recalling it as often as I found it wandered from Him . . . I made this my business as much all the day long as at the appointed times of prayer; for at all times, every hour, every minute, even in the height of my business, I drove away

from my mind everything that was capable of interrupting my thought of God . . . I have found great advantages by it . . . by often repeating these acts, they become habitual, and the presence of God rendered it were natural to us.[20]

Such conversation with God brought Brother Lawrence much joy and ecstasy:

And I make it my business only to persevere in His holy presence, wherein I keep myself by a simple attention, and a general fond regard to God, which I may call an actual presence of God; or, to speak better, an habitual, silent, and secret conversation of the soul with God, which often causes me joys and raptures inwardly, and sometimes also outwardly, so great that I am forced to use means to moderate them and prevent their appearance to others . . . There is not in the world a kind of life more sweet and delightful than that of continual conversation with God. Those only can comprehend it who practice and experience it . . . while I am so with Him I fear nothing, but the least turning from Him is insupportable.[21]

Brother Lawrence advises us that, when practising the presence of God, we should be *gentle* with our mind – 'that we must do our business faithfully, without trouble or disquiet, recalling our mind to God mildly, and with tranquility, as often as we find it wandering from Him'.[22] He also suggests:

think often on God, by day, by night, in your business, and even in your diversions. He is always near you and with you; leave Him not alone. You would think it rude to leave a friend alone who came to visit you; why, then, must God be neglected? Do not, then, forget Him, but think on Him often, adore Him continually. We must make our heart a spiritual temple, wherein to adore Him incessantly . . . If we knew how much He loves us, we should always be ready to receive equally and with indifference from His hand the sweet and the bitter.[23]

Another inspiring source for the practice of God's presence is the poems of the eighth-century female Muslim mystic Rabi'a, whose deep sense of love and adoration for God is reflected in her beautiful poetry. Here are a few examples:

O God, my whole occupation and all my desire in this world, of all worldly things, is to remember Thee, and in the world to come, of all things of the world to come is to meet Thee.[24]

O God . . . Give the goods of this world to Your enemies – Give the treasures of Paradise to Your friends – But as for me – You are all I need.

O God! If I adore You out of fear of Hell, burn me in Hell! If I adore You out of desire for Paradise, lock me out of Paradise. But if I adore You for Yourself alone, Do not deny to me Your eternal beauty.[25]

Your hope in my heart is the rarest treasure
Your Name on my tongue is the sweetest word
My choicest hours Are the hours I spend with You – O God,
I can't live in this world
Without remembering You
How can I endure the next world
Without seeing Your face?[26]

Rabi'a – Rabi'a – how did you climb so high?
'I did it by saying: "Let me hide in You
From everything that distracts me from You,
From everything that comes in my way
When I want to run to You." '[27]

Yet another great resource for the practice of God's presence is 'Abdu'l-Bahá's *Memorials of the Faithful,* which contains inspiring stories of some of the early disciples of Bahá'u'lláh. These individuals attempted to live a God-centred life. Among these disciples was:

Ḥájí Mullá Mihdíy-i-Yazdí . . . persevering in his devotions, known for holy practices . . . He spent most of his time repeating communes . . . He was an eminent soul, with his heart fixed on the beauty of God.[28]

On the nature and the outcome of living a God-conscious life, 'Abdu'l-Bahá said:

> . . . the heart must be turned always towards God, no matter what the work is . . . We are like a piece of iron in the midst of the fire which becomes heated to such a degree that it partakes of the nature of the fire and gives out the same effect to all it touches – so is the soul that is always turned towards God, and filled with the spirit.[29]

'Abdu'l-Bahá is reported to have taught a group of western pilgrims how to live a life that is focused on Bahá'u'lláh as God's Messenger for this day:

> Advance always in the Kingdom of Bahá'u'lláh; make always thy heart occupied by the mentioning of Bahá'u'lláh; consider that only in your eyes is Bahá'u'lláh; in your heart is Bahá'u'lláh; in your inmost heart is Bahá'u'lláh. If you fall into trouble, say 'Yá-Bahá'u'l-Abhá;' . . . Even when you may be in your work, mention 'Yá-Bahá'u'l -Abhá.'[30]

How to Practise the Presence of God?

We can start practising the presence of God by using physical means to remind ourselves – such as by wearing a wrist band or putting stickers in various places in our house – that God is always with us as a loving companion. Therefore, we are not alone. Even though we don't see Him, He is with us, sees us, hears our prayers, watches over us and protects us. All we have to do is to turn to Him in prayer, supplication, praise and glorification, and thanksgiving. Like a flower that turns to the sun, we can turn to Him and invoke His Name so that He can guide and protect us, help draw us closer to Him, and purify the mirror of our hearts from negative thoughts and feelings.

Over time and with daily practice, God-consciousness becomes a habit. Visualizing His presence as a loving companion will gradually strengthen the reflection of our innate heavenly qualities such as love, kindness and patience. Practising mindfulness of God's presence will also protect us from negative thoughts and emotions, and from engaging in unproductive or undesirable behaviours. To close this chapter, here are a few more quotations from prayers revealed by Bahá'u'lláh on the mindfulness of God:

I beg of Thee . . . to guard mine eyes from beholding aught beside Thee.[31]

. . . grant that I may, at all times, be wholly dissolved in Thee . . .[32]

. . . let Thy remembrance be my companion, and Thy love my aim, and Thy face my goal, and Thy name my lamp, and Thy wish my desire, and Thy pleasure my delight.[33]

10

METTA MEDITATION

O Friend! In the garden of thy heart plant naught but the rose
of love.

Bahá'u'lláh[1]

The word *metta* is a Pali[2] word that means 'loving-kindness'.[3] In
Buddhism, there is much emphasis on acquiring this virtue – so
much so that a whole meditation practice is formed around it. It
seems that all the other virtues such as wisdom and compassion,
the acquiring of which Buddha has also emphasized, find their
fruition in the practice of loving-kindness toward ourselves and
the world. The assumption is that if we adopt such an attitude and
manifest it in our thoughts and deeds, we will arrive at peace in
both our inner and outer world.

At the core of metta meditation is the notion of love and its
power to unite all humans and bring us happiness. As we go
through life's journey, many of us yearn for the capacity to truly
love and feel connected to others. Within the Buddhist tradition, metta meditation is believed to teach us how to manifest the
joyful and radiant heart that is enshrined within our innermost
being and allow it to radiate out to the world. Supporters of metta
meditation believe it also helps us to cultivate other qualities such
as compassion, equanimity and sympathetic joy. Additionally,
the practice is expected to help us overcome the false sense of
'separateness' from others. It is this feeling that brings us sadness,
fear, loneliness and alienation. Consistent engagement in metta
meditation can help us replace these negative feelings with a
genuine sense of interconnectedness. This, in turn, can generate

confidence, security, unity, and ultimately happiness.[4]

The Buddha taught that negative forces such as greed, anger, sorrow, hate and guilt could temporarily restrain the positive forces of love, compassion and wisdom that we inherently possess. However, these negative forces don't have the power to permanently destroy the positive forces within us. This indicates the ultimate supremacy of positive over negative forces and their ability to uproot negative forces. For instance, love can uproot hate because it is a more powerful force. Hate can restrain love for a while but it cannot destroy love.[5]

The word metta also means friendship and friendliness. This compassionate form of meditation teaches us how to tap into our innate reservoir of love so we can become a friend to ourselves and to the world. Among the other benefits of metta meditation are an increase in self-respect, care and consideration for others and recognition of the importance of living a harmonious existence with all forms of life on the planet.

In metta meditation, we gently repeat phrases that express worthwhile and enduring wishes, first for ourselves and then for others. The phrases we choose should focus on things that are truly significant to us. For instance we can say, 'may I be happy', 'may I be peaceful', 'may I be healthy', 'may I be healed', 'may I live with ease', or 'may I live in peace'.[6]

A typical metta meditation session takes between 20 and 30 minutes.[7] To start a session, sit comfortably with your eyes closed while you focus on your breathing for a few minutes. Then, visualize yourself at any age and in any surroundings with which you feel comfortable. Choose three or four phrases that convey your deepest wish for yourself and gently repeat them over and over again. For instance, picture yourself as a mother would hold her child and, with love and gentleness,[8] repeat these phrases silently to yourself for about 10 minutes: 'May I be well, may I be happy, may all things go well for me.'[9] If your mind begins to wander, lovingly bring it back to the metta phrases. Sending ourselves care may sound selfish and egotistical, but in reality it is not. We can only love others if we first manifest love and self-respect to ourselves. Imagine the opposite. If you hate yourself and have little or no self-respect or confidence, would you be able to manifest *genuine* love and respect towards others? If you feel any discomfort arising, just let the feeling pass by like clouds in the sky and take a few breaths.

Next, visualize a person who is important to you. Sometimes in Buddhism such a person is referred to as the 'benefactor'. The benefactor could be a family member, a friend or a colleague. The traditional teachings of Buddhism encourage practitioners to begin with someone who is still living and who is not an object of sexual desire. Think of their inner goodness, their kindness to you and their contributions to the world. Then as you are saying their name, or bringing their image to mind, or simply getting a feel for their presence with you, silently and slowly send them the same metta phrases you have sent yourself. For instance, say: 'May you be well, may you be happy, may all things go well for you.'[10] It is all right to change the benefactor over time.

Now, picture someone you may or may not know quite as well, a 'neutral person'. Then send them the same metta you sent to your family member, friend or colleague. It would be helpful to choose someone you see occasionally. This way, the metta meditation will help you experience a sense of interconnectedness with them. Over time, you may develop warmth and care toward this other person even if you have never said a word to them. This is a good way of breaking down the barriers between us and others.

Finally, if there are people for whom you have negative feelings, bring them to mind and send them the same metta you sent to the other two groups. This last step is a very powerful stage in your metta meditation practice because it will help you transform your conditional love for others into an unconditional one. Here, you learn an incredibly powerful lesson: that, like the sun, true love can and should shine on everyone and everything.

One way to do this part of your metta meditation is to look for a small quality that you like about them – maybe their smile – and bring your attention to the particular quality. See if you can remember a kind thing he or she has done in the past. Focus on that positive thought as long as you can, and then see if your feelings have changed.

When you are done with your metta for this last group, sit quietly for a few minutes and enjoy the positive feelings you have experienced by being loving and compassionate toward all things. As you leave your meditation place with a smile on your face, have a firm resolve to carry those positive feelings with you in all that you do and say in the course of the day.[11]

There is now scientific evidence that we can use metta meditation to train our brains to suppress feelings of fear and anxiety. Metta meditation can achieve this by impacting the hippocampus, a major component of the brain in humans and mammals. The hippocampus plays a significant role in consolidating information from short-term to long-term memory. Unfortunately, it is also the first part of the brain that can be damaged by tension, anxiety and wrath. Individuals with a damaged hippocampus are unable to form or retain new memories, which makes them susceptible to ailments such as Alzheimer's disease and amnesia. The studies by Andrew Newberg and Mark Waldman have shown that metta meditation can help us suppress negative feelings that could damage our hippocampus and can even help us grow new nerve cells in that region of the brain.[12]

In his book *Essential Spirituality*, Dr Roger Walsh suggests another meditation for cultivating the quality of love, which he refers to as 'recalling loving people'. Here is what he suggests:

Make yourself comfortable in a place where you can sit quietly without interruption for several minutes. Take time to relax and breathe slowly and deeply. You might wish to imagine that you are breathing in and out through the center of your chest, since this fosters feelings of warmth and love. Then bring to mind people you know or know of who are exceptionally loving. They might include family members, friends, wise people you have met, or saints and sages you have heard of. Take a moment to think of each person. As you do so, bring to mind the gifts they give. Consider their personalities and behavior. What qualities make them so kind and loving?

Notice your state of mind as you reflect on these people. You may find yourself feeling grateful and loving because, simply by directing attention to specific people, we begin to feel the qualities they express. This is an important lesson: those people we give attention to have powerful effects on us. Associate with angry people and anger surges up within us; think of loving people and love arises. The Buddha warned: 'Do not look for bad company or live with people who do not care. Find friends who love the truth.' [13]

Baha'u'llah gave similar advice in his *Hidden Words*:

O My Son! The company of the ungodly increaseth sorrow, whilst fellowship with the righteous cleanseth the rust from off the heart. He that seeketh to commune with God, let him betake himself to the companionship of His loved ones; and he that desireth to hearken unto the word of God, let him give ear to the words of His chosen ones. [14]

A similar practice for cultivating love for oneself has been suggested by Sharon Salzberg in her book *Loving-kindness*. She calls this exercise, 'remembering the good within you'. She states that through this exercise, we can begin to develop happiness by rejoicing in our own innate goodness.

To do this meditation, sit comfortably and as you close your eyes, focus your attention on the sensation of breathing for a few minutes. Now for the next ten to fifteen minutes, bring to mind a kind action you have done or a kind statement you have made to another person to alleviate their discomfort. If something comes to your mind, such as a time when you did a favour for a friend that made them happy – or even when you simply said a few comforting words to someone in need of consolation – then allow the joy that comes with a memory like that to warm your heart and give you an 'inner' or even an outer smile.

If nothing comes to mind, simply bring your focus to a

characteristic or a talent that you have and for which you are grateful. Maybe you are a naturally kind and loving person. Maybe you have a zest for teaching and are a great teacher. Maybe you have talent in music or some kind of art or a gift in another area. If still nothing comes to mind, bring your attention to your desire for happiness and focus on this urge within you.

As with any other type of meditation, when thoughts and emotions arise, gently bring your attention – without any guilt or judgement – to your practice. Simply let distracting and unwelcome thoughts fly across the sky of your mind.

According to Salzberg, it is not the goal of such reflection to make us egotistical and conceited. On the contrary, such an exercise should be a commitment to our own joy as we see our happiness as the foundation for closeness with all life. It should fill our hearts with happiness and love for ourselves and lead us to an ever-growing sense of self-respect.

There are still other practices for cultivating a sense of love and self-respect for ourselves. Among them are keeping a 'Kindness journal' and 'Practising a day of kindness'.

Keeping a Kindness Journal

Keeping a kindness journal is another way to cultivate the seeds of love and kindness within our souls. To do this, get a beautiful notebook. On pages on one side of the notebook, write a number of inspiring quotations from the scriptures of the world's religions on the virtues of kindness and love. Such powerful words have regenerative power and can make us a 'new creation'. On pages facing them we can provide examples of the times we have practised kindness and love in our words and deeds and the way we felt afterwards.

There are many advantages to keeping a kindness journal. For one thing, we feel good about ourselves and life in general as we write in it. It also helps with the development of a healthy self-esteem as we focus our attention on what really matters in life – namely, showing love and kindness to our fellow human beings.

Such a unifying ideal is at the core of all the great world religions. Furthermore, keeping a kindness journal can be of great value when we encounter tests and trials in life. Reading the accounts of our good deeds will give us a sense of satisfaction with ourselves and our lives. It helps us relive those moments and warms our hearts, thus inspiring us to continue on the path of kindness and love.

A Day of Kindness

A complementary practice to nurturing the quality of love and kindness within our soul is to devote an entire day to practising kindness in our thoughts, words and deeds. In the course of that specific day, we avoid allowing resentful and negative thoughts to linger in our minds and, as they appear, we gently move to more productive thoughts with an 'inner smile'. We see to it that the words we utter in the course of that day are mindful, masterful and beautiful, like paintings on a canvas. Finally, we make an attempt to practise acts of kindness, such as visiting or calling a friend who is in need of comfort and encouragement.

Practices like metta meditation, recalling loving people, remembering the good within you, keeping a kindness journal, and a day of kindness are great tools for developing this much-needed virtue in ourselves. All the great religions of the world teach their adherents about the significance of love. This includes the Bahá'í Faith, which also encourages the development of compassion and loving-kindness towards others:

> We should . . . occupy ourselves in offering prayers for the good of all.[15]

> I charge you all that each one of you concentrate all the thoughts of your heart on love and unity.[16]

In the world of existence there is no more powerful magnet than the magnet of love.[17]

Each sees in the other the Beauty of God reflected in the soul, and finding this point of similarity, they are attracted to one another in love. This love will make all men the waves of one sea, this love will make them all the stars of one heaven and the fruits of one tree. This love will bring the realization of true accord, the foundation of real unity.[18]

Do not be content with showing friendship in words alone, let your heart burn with loving kindness for all who may cross your path.[19]

Strive to attain a station of absolute love one toward another. By the absence of love, enmity increases. By the exercise of love, love strengthens and enmities dwindle away.[20]

An Example of Practising Compassion

In the Bahá'í Writings, Bahá'u'lláh teaches us that one of the main reasons for the advent of the Prophets is make us aware of the 'trust of God' that is 'latent in the reality' of our souls.

He [God] hath sent forth His Messengers, His Prophets and chosen ones that they might acquaint the people with the divine purpose underlying the revelation of Books and the raising up of Messengers, and that everyone may become aware of the trust of God which is latent in the reality of every soul.[21]

Many of us find it easier to be kind to others than to ourselves! We try hard to be loving, caring, understanding, forgiving, compassionate and patient to our children, our family members and friends, but find it much harder to treat ourselves with the same positive strokes. Instead of realistic assessments of our strengths and areas of improvement, we often tend to focus on our weaknesses alone and become very critical of our shortcomings. If you find yourself guilty of this, as I did with myself, you can overcome it by remembering the 'child within you' who is the 'trust of God' and needs to be loved and respected. Regardless of your age, that inner child needs care, compassion, nurturing and forgiveness. You are still responsible for the spiritual growth and happiness of the child within you, even if you are in your 60s or 70s. Bring that inner child 'out' by placing a physical sign of him or her somewhere in your home, preferably in your meditation room or meditation corner where you can look at it in the right frame of mind. This is what we have done as a family and here is how it happened.

I had started looking at a baby picture of myself daily as a reminder of the 'inner child' within me when, on my birthday, my husband surprised me with a simple but very thoughtful gift. He had ordered a mug with a picture of me from when I was six months old. I decided to replicate the mug idea with two more: one for my husband and one for our son Adib. The three mugs are now sitting side-by-side on a table in our meditation room (see photograph section).

This visual symbol of the 'inner child' enables my family to regularly reinforce in us the need to treat each other with love, compassion, care and patience, and reminds us that, ultimately, each of us is responsible for the spiritual development of that 'trust of God' within us.

11

MANTRA MEDITATION (JAPA MEDITATION)

> ... the desire of our soul is to thy name, and to the remembrance of thee. *Isaiah 26:8*

In *The Mantram Handbook*, Eknath Easwaran defines *mantra* as follows:

> The Mantram (mantra) is a short, powerful spiritual formula for the highest power that we can conceive of.[1]

Mantra meditation is an easy yet powerful way of practising God's presence in our life. Be sure to choose the mantra that is most appealing to you.[2] For instance, if you are a Hindu, you might choose to meditate on the name of a Hindu deity such as *Rama* or *Krishna*. If you are a Christian, you could choose to invoke the name of *Christ*. A person of Jewish faith might choose the word *Adonai* (Lord) as the focal point of his or her meditation.

Mantra meditation is a popular method across several religious traditions, including Hinduism, Tibetan Buddhism, Orthodox Christianity and Sufism. More recently, this approach has also been adopted by those practising Transcendental Meditation and the Christian centering prayer. A story about the Indian mystic Ramakrishna (1836–86) recounts that he used various meditation techniques for twelve years, but when someone asked for his opinion on the best approach to meditation, he recommended only meditating on the Name of God.[3]

Among the most well-known Hindu mantras are *Hare Rama Hare Rama, Hare Krishna Hare Krishna* and *Om Namah Shivaya* (homage to Shiva who transforms negativity).[4]

In the Buddhist tradition, the mantra *Om Mani Padme Hum* (Jewel in the Heart of the Lotus) signifies the jewel or the capacity we all have for the attainment of enlightenment.[5]

The adherents of *Pure Land Buddhism* may use the name of Buddha Amida or Amita[6] for their mantra.

In the Jewish mystical tradition, the earliest explicit reference to a form of mantra meditation can be found in Merkava mysticism that dates back to the Talmudic period. Here, a meditator is expected to repeat a Name of God, or a phrase that consists of certain mystical terms, 120 times. In some Kabbalistic schools, the meditator used a verse from the Bible, the Talmud or the Zohar[7] as his or her mantra. For instance, in 16th-century Safed – a city in the northern district of today's Israel – a technique known as *gerushin*[8] was practised, which entailed the repetition of a biblical verse over and over much like a mantra meditation. This technique would not only help the meditator attain to a higher level of consciousness; it would also provide him with a more profound understanding of the verse itself. As for the best approach to mantra meditation within a Jewish paradigm, Aryeh Kaplan prescribes the repetition of the phrase 'Master of the Universe' used by a famous Hasidic leader, Rabbi Nachman of Bratslav (1772–1811) as an excellent phrase for any Jew who is interested in this technique.[9]

In Christianity, based on the biblical verse 'Pray unceasingly' (1 Thess. 5:17), some early Christian mystics began to use the *'Prayer of Jesus'* or the *'Prayer of the Heart'*, which is: 'Lord Jesus Christ, have mercy upon me', to quiet their minds and draw closer to Jesus.

The practice of repeating the Prayer of Jesus became known as *hesychasm*, which comes from a Greek word meaning *prayerful quietness*. Monks were told to repeat this prayer over and over with undivided attention while resisting all intrusive thoughts. The practice was supposed to lead to inner calm and help the mystic draw nearer to Christ.[10]

Today, a well-known approach to mantra meditation in Christianity is the practice of the Centering Prayer, which has its roots in *The Cloud of Unknowing*, a Christian mystical work dating back to the 14th century CE. In this particular type of meditation, the meditator is expected to choose a sacred word as a symbol of her 'intention to consent to God's presence and action within'.[11] Then, sitting comfortably and with her eyes closed, the person silently repeats the sacred word. If any intruding thoughts enter her mind, the meditator is expected to 'return ever-so-gently to the sacred word'. At the end of the session, he or she should remain in silence with her eyes closed for a couple of minutes.[12]

In Islam, the practice of *zikr*[13] (or *dhikr*) is at the heart of Sufism (Muslim mysticism). It is the practice of invoking the Name of God or 'remembering' Him. The aim of a Sufi is to keep his mind pure by engaging in constant *Zikr* through 'the repetitive recitation of divine names or short, sacred formulas, often derived from the Qur'án . . . the aim of *Zikr* is to bring about an unveiling of our spiritual self. It is the act of polishing the heart in order to make it a perfect mirror reflecting the light of God.'[14] The most common *zikr* in Sufism is *La ilaha illa' llah* (لا إله إلا الله), which means 'There is no god but God'.

Through the practice of *zikr*, the Sufi tries to overcome the mind's natural state of inattention. Ultimately, as he gains mastery over his mind, he can become focused on God at all times.[15] *Zikr* is the fundamental exercise for opening one's inner eyes to see the unity of existence. The nature of such practice varies from one Sufi order to another; however, such spiritual discipline is of paramount importance in all of them. Sufis find plenty of support for the practice of *zikr* in the Qur'án.[16] Within the Sufi belief system, *zikr* is as essential for the heart of the believer as water is for the fish.[17] It is also regarded as the gateway to God's love. Through the practice of *Zikr*, the believer can experience His presence during worship. In *The Naqshbandi Sufi Tradition Guidebook of Daily Practices and Devotions*, the author describes the merits of *zikr* in the following manner:

Dhikr, or remembrance of God (Allah), is the most excellent act of God's servants . . . It is the most praiseworthy practice to earn God's good-pleasure . . . It is the . . . essence of the science of faith . . . the foremost worship . . . There are no restrictions on the method, frequency, or timing of *Dhikr* whatsoever.[18]

How To Do Mantra Meditation

Thou dost keep him in perfect peace, whose mind is stayed on Thee.[19]

Sit with your back straight and your eyes closed. Use prayer beads to help you concentrate on your mantra. Begin the practice by repeating the mantra you have chosen out loud for a while, followed by a period of whispering it, and finally ending with mental recitation of the mantra. Giving your mind such variety will prevent boredom and weariness. Saying the mantra aloud will help block the sounds and distractions you might face. The most potent part of the mantra meditation is to repeat the mantra *mentally* because it calls for a very focused concentration. Feel free to alternate when necessary, especially when you encounter drowsiness.[20]

If the mantra of your choice is a Name of God, invoke His Name with love and adoration. It should never be forced, rushed or contrived. Rather, it should be invoked gently, slowly, attentively and gracefully.[21] During the session, you can use various visualizations to enhance your practice. For instance, 'meditate like a mountain'. To do so, imagine you are sitting like a mountain. Feel your weight and your presence, and visualize sitting silently under the rays of the sun that symbolizes God's radiance.[22]

When the meditation session is over, instead of leaving your sacred space immediately, sit quietly with your eyes closed. Then, while visualizing Him in your mind as a glorious, effulgent Light, reach out to Him and ask Him to stay with you and to bestow upon you the grace to carry on, calling on His Blessed Name in the course of the day in your heart and in your mind.

When to Say the Mantra

> When a man falls in love with a human being, it is impossible for him to keep from mentioning the name of his beloved. How much more difficult is it to keep from mentioning the Name of God when one has come to love Him . . . The spiritual man finds no delight in anything save in commemoration of God.[23]

The repetition of a mantra is like a broom that sweeps our mind free of trash.[24] The purifying effect of mantra is beautifully illustrated in this Muslim hadith:

> Everything has a polish, and the polish of hearts is _dhikr_ of God.[25]

In the Qur'án, God says:

> . . . never tire of remembering Me.[26]

Therefore, in addition to setting aside a time for mantra meditation as a daily practice for the discipline of the mind, we can look for opportunities in the course of the day to repeat the mantra. For instance, repeat it silently in your mind as you go for a walk, while you are waiting for your turn at the doctor's office or grocery store, or for the traffic light to change. Say it when you clean your house or do your laundry or wash the dishes. A great way to start the day is by saying the mantra as you open your eyes in the morning while feeling God's presence around you.

This practice can be repeated at night as you put your head on the pillow. Falling sleep in His Name is a great habit to develop. It might also help you sleep better! Another occasion to repeat the mantra is when you experience negative thoughts or feelings like anger, hatred, restlessness, hopelessness, fear or anxiety. So the next time you encounter any of these feelings, close your eyes and, with your heart turned towards God, repeat your mantra silently in the mind while drawing upon His immense power to replace those feelings with peace, composure and assurance. Over time, the mantra can gradually turn into a familiar friend whose company you will really come to enjoy.

Illness is another opportunity for reciting the mantra. When we are unwell many of us spend a good deal of time and energy dwelling on our symptoms. We worry about the seriousness of our disease and about when we will recover. We don't realize that this uneasiness can actually impede the healing process. On the contrary, when our mind is at ease, the power of His Name will help release our body's natural healing forces to help bring us back to health.[27] The mantra is most effective when we repeat it quietly in our mind[28] with as much focus as we can possibly muster. At times, we may have to say the mantra out loud a few times to get started.

Having a part of our mind focused on our mantra as an ongoing practice will help us stay peaceful and centred, in spite of the daily challenges that come our way. The mantra will also be of great assistance in gaining mastery over our mind.[29] Repetition of the mantra has a cumulative effect, and with continued practice it gains power: 'When the Mantra can be repeated throughout the day, God-consciousness will permeate one's life.'[30]

Invoking the Name of God as the main instrument for drawing closer to Him and living in His presence has been suggested by most saints and spiritual teachers throughout the world. Calling on His Name with loving devotion and faith in its power makes our mind steady and calm, conserves our much-needed energy, and helps us acquire flexibility and confidence. It will help us become less judgemental about ourselves and others, and it acts as a shield against selfish desires. With so many benefits, you may want to consider teaching your children this spiritual discipline when they are young. That way, they will grow up knowing that they are always safe in the shelter of His Name.[31]

On practising the invocation of the Name of God as a means of living in His Presence and attaining peace and spiritual felicity, Swami Chidananda (1916–2008) said the following:

The secret of growing into spiritual consciousness is to CLING to THE DIVINE NAME day and night. All things will pass away. But the Divine Name reigns supreme forever. Engage yourself in repeating the Divine Name. Learn to surrender your little ego and attachment at the feet of the Divine. Feel the Presence of God constantly with you at all times, at all places and in all things that you do. Do you not see that God is your eternal companion? Can you not feel that He sits with you when you sit; He walks with you when you walk? . . . God permeates every thought, feeling, sentiment and mood of yours. Inside and outside, the Divine Power alone sustains you. Awaken to those facts and live in God . . . For this, again I tell you, cling to the Divine Name . . . The Divine Name is your greatest treasure . . . It will awaken God-consciousness in you . . . This is the easy way to a life in God. Come, friend, waste not your precious time. Repeat the Name . . . Live in God. Attain Supreme Blessedness.[32]

If the repetition of the mantra from the heart becomes a daily practice, before too long the mantra repeats itself on its own, more like

a top spinning inside which every now and then needs just a flick to keep it going. Eventually, it will go on with no need of encouragement, as in the case of Saint Kabir, who said, 'Ram practices my *japa* [repetition of God's name], while I sit relaxed.' It's a blissful moment when you notice that happening.[33]

In the following well-known Christian source, we can find more on the fruit of this practice:

I implore you therefore not to withdraw your hearts from God, but to watch them and guard them by constant remembrance of our Lord Jesus Christ, until the name of our Lord is deeply rooted in your heart and you cease to think of aught but glorifying the Lord in you . . . For as the more the rain pours down upon the earth, the more it softens the earth; so too the holy Name of Christ, when it is invoked by us without thoughts, the more constantly we call upon it, the more it softens the earth of our heart, and fills it with joy and delight.[34]

Finally, the remembrance of God as a means of drawing closer to Him can be seen in this well-known Muslim hadith:

> As my servant thinks about Me so will I be for him. I am with him if he will remember Me. If he calls on Me in himself I will call him in Myself, and if he calls on Me in a group of people, I mention him in a better group in My presence. If he approaches Me one handspan, I will approach him one arm's length; if he approaches Me one arm's length, I will approach him by a cubit; if he comes to Me walking, I will come to him running.[35]

The Power of the Name of God

In a prayer revealed by Bahá'u'lláh we read:

> Armed with the Power of Thy name nothing can ever hurt me, and with Thy love in my heart all the world's afflictions can in no wise alarm me. [36]

The significance of the Name of God and its immense power has been emphasized in the sacred literature of the world's religions:

> I am easily attainable, O Arjuna, by that ever steadfast yogi who always thinks of Me and whose mind does not go elsewhere.[37]

> The name of the Lord is a strong tower; The righteous man runs into it and is safe.[38]

> Save me, O God, by Thy name.[39]

And whatever you do, in word or deed, do everything in the name of the Lord Jesus . . . [40]

Whatever you ask in my name, I will do it, that the Father may be glorified in the Son; if you ask anything in my name, I will do it.[41]

To happiness [in the life to come] will indeed attain he who attains to purity [in this world], and remembers his Sustainer's name, and prays [unto Him].[42]

The remembrance of Thee is a healing medicine to the hearts of such as have drawn nigh unto Thy court.[43]

Thy Name is my healing, O my God, and remembrance of Thee is my remedy.[44]

His Name is indeed the healing medicine for every illness . . . It is the sovereign remedy.[45]

I beseech Thee by Thy Name, whereby everyone is enabled to attain the object of his desire.[46]

I implore Thee, O my Lord, by Thy Name . . . which Thou didst ordain to be the most great Instrument binding Thee to Thy servants.[47]

I beseech Thee . . . by Thy Name through which Thou hast . . . guided all them that yearn after Thee into the Paradise of Thy nearness, and Thy Presence . . . [48]

Through habitual practice of mantra meditation, God's Name could give you detachment and courage – qualities that will give you strength in times of trial. The repetition of His Name from the heart is a sure way of drawing closer to Him. Mahatma Gandhi (1869-1948) was a devout believer in the tremendous power of the Name of God, which to him was Ramanama.[49] The use of a mantra by a renowned politician such as Gandhi is inspiring to even the most pragmatic individuals, who might ordinarily leave such practices to religious people. He said:

> Even if I am killed, I will not give up repeating the names of Rama and Rahim[50] which mean to me the same God. With these names on my lips I will die cheerfully.[51]

On the power of the Name of God, Gandhi said that each repetition

> has a new meaning, each repetition carries you nearer and nearer to God. This is a concrete fact, and I may tell you that you are here talking to no theorist, but to one who has experienced what he says every minute of his life, so much so that it is easier for the life to stop than for this incessant process to stop. It is a definite need of the soul.[52]

Further, he said:

> The mantra [the Name of God] becomes one's staff of life and carries one through every ordeal.[53]

Gandhi's experience with God's Name, which to him was the most precious possession, began when he was a child:

> I am a stranger to yogic practices. The practice I follow is a practice I learnt in my childhood from my nurse. I was afraid of ghosts. She used to say to me : 'There are no ghosts, but if you are afraid, repeat Ramanama.' What I learnt in my childhood has become a huge thing in my mental firmament. It is a sun that has brightened my darkest hour. A Christian may find the same solace from the repetition of the name of Jesus, and a Muslim from the name of Allah. All these things have the same implications and they produce identical results under

identical circumstances. Only the repetition must not be a lip expression, but part of your very being.[54]

He also wrote:

I have said that to take Ramanama from the heart means deriving help from an incomparable power. The atom bomb is as nothing compared with it. This power is capable of removing all pain. There is no doubt whatsoever that Ramanama contains all the power that is attributed to it. No one can by mere wishing enshrine Ramanama in his heart. Untiring effort is required, as also patience. What an amount of labor and patience have been lavished by men to acquire the nonexistent philosopher's stone? Surely, God's name is of infinitely richer value. With my hand on my breast, I can say that not a minute in my life am I forgetful of God . . . One has, therefore to appear before him in all one's meekness, empty-handed, and in a spirit of full surrender, and he enables you to stand before the whole world and protects you from all harm.[55]

On the healing power of God's Name, Gandhi said:

No matter what the ailment from which a man may be suffering, recitation of Ramanama from the heart is the sure cure.[56]

Gandhi believed that if we recite God's Name from our heart continuously in the course of the day, it will ultimately keep repeating itself during our sleep, and through the grace of God we will be endowed with a sound mind, body and soul. He called God's Name 'the unfailing panacea for all ills'.[57]

Within the Christian tradition, the practice of repeating the Name of God for the purpose of purification and assistance was common among many Christian saints. For instance, St Francis of Assisi is believed to have repeated 'My God and my all' throughout the night. Another saint, Bruno, is said to have loved contemplating and praising God in the short phrase, 'O goodness of God'.[58]

Bahá: The Greatest Name Of God

> O Peoples of the world! He Who is the Most Great Name is
> come, on the part of the Ancient King.[59]

The word *Bahá*, an Arabic word meaning 'glory' or 'splendour',
has its roots in Shí'i Islam, where one of the most significant
occurrences of this word in Shí'i literature is in a dawn prayer
(Du'a al-Sahar) attributed to the fifth of the Twelve Shí'i Imams,
Muhammad al-Baqir (677–732 CE). The eighth Imam, Imam
Reza (d. 818 CE), who transmitted this invocatory prayer, believed
that it contained God's 'Greatest Name' *(al-ism al-a'zam)*. The
prayer was to be recited at dawn during Ramadan, the month of
fasting for Muslims.[60] It begins with the following verse:

> O my God! I beseech Thee by Thy Bahá' (Splendour) at its
> most splendid (abhá) for all Thy Splendour (bahá) is truly
> resplendent (bahiyy). I, verily, O my God! beseech Thee by
> the fullness of Thy Splendour (bahá').[61]

Bahá'u'lláh refers to this dawn prayer, as Stephen Lambden explains:

> There exists an Arabic prayer of Bahá'u'lláh – headed 'In the
> name of God, al-Abhá– which opens with reference to the
> Shí'í Dawn Prayer, the first line of which it subsequently
> quotes. By means of this *Dawn Prayer,* God had been suppli-
> cated, Bahá'u'lláh meditates, by the tongue of His Messengers
> *(rusul),* beseeched through the 'tongues of those who are nigh
> unto God'. All, in fact, were commanded to recite it at dawn-
> times for it contains the 'Greatest Name' and is a protection
> against being veiled from that Name (Bahá) which is the 'orna-
> ment' of God's 'Self'.[62]

In addition to the dawn prayer, there are many Muslim traditions *(hadith)*, attributed to both the Prophet Muhammad and
the Twelve Shí'í Imams, that contain the word 'Bahá'. There was

also a hadith that God's Greatest Name was hidden and had tremendous power. Shí'i Imams were believed to have knowledge of
this Name and to draw immense power from it. On this subject
the first Imam, 'Alí, is reported to have said:

> Our Lord has given to us the knowledge of the Greatest Name,
> through which, were we to want to, we would rend asunder
> the heavens and the earth and paradise and hell; through it we
> ascend to heaven and we travel to the east and to the west until
> we reach the Throne (of God) and sit upon it before God and
> He gives us all things, even the heavens, the earth, the sun,
> moon and stars, the mountains, the trees, the paths, heaven
> and hell.[63]

There are many occurrences of the term Bahá in both the Bábí
and Bahá'í Holy Texts. For instance, in the Báb's *Qayyúmu'l-Asmá'*
it occurs fourteen times, while in another book, the *Kitáb-i Panj
Sha'an* (Book of the Five Grades), He uses the word Bahá'u'lláh
along with different derivatives of the word Bahá many times.[64]

Significance of the Greatest Name of God

Shoghi Effendi, the Guardian of the Bahá'í Faith, elaborates on
the significance of the Greatest Name:

> The Greatest Name is the Name of Bahá'u'lláh. 'Yá Bahá'u'l-
> Abhá' is an invocation meaning: 'O Thou Glory of Glories'!
> 'Alláh-u-Abhá' is a greeting which means: 'God the All-Glo-
> rious'. Both refer to Bahá'u'lláh. By Greatest Name is meant
> that Baha'u'llah has appeared in God's Greatest Name, in
> other words, that He is the Supreme Manifestation of God.[65]

> [Shoghi Effendi] also wishes me to inform you that the symbol
> of the Greatest Name represents an invocation which can be
> translated either as 'O Glory of Glories' or 'O Glory of the
> All-Glorious'. . . [66]

The following Tablet known as the 'Tablet of the Greatest Name' was revealed by 'Abdu'l-Bahá:

> O ye beloved friends of God and handmaids of the Merciful!
>
> Call ye to mind the blessed Name of our peerless Beloved, the Abhá Beauty, in an uplifting spirit of unbounded ecstasy and delight, then unloose your tongues in His praise in such wise that the realm of the heart may be purged from the woes and sorrows of the world of water and clay, that the great heights of spiritual perception may be unveiled before your eyes, that the glorious signs of His Divine Unity may shine resplendent, a fresh outpouring of His grace may stream forth, and a liberal effusion of celestial confirmations may be vouchsafed unto you.
>
> His Name is indeed the healing medicine for every illness, and imparteth warmth unto those starving with cold. It is the sovereign remedy and the supreme talisman. It is the source of life in both worlds, and of salvation unto such as have gone astray. Today this hallowed Name serveth as a shield for all mankind, and as a veritable refuge for the children of men. It is the wondrous accent of the Lord of Mercy, and His celestial melody.
>
> Wherefore, O faithful friends, raise ye the triumphal cry of Yá Bahá'u'l-Abhá! O ye who yearn after the Beauty of the Almighty! Lift up your faces toward the Supreme Horizon. Rest not, even for a moment. Breathe not a single breath save in remembrance of His love and in recognition of His grace, in the promulgation of His Utterances and the vindication of His Testimonies.
>
> Verily, this is the Magnet of divine confirmations. This is the mighty Force which will surely attract heavenly assistance.[67]

Within a Bahá'í framework, the word 'Bahá' can be viewed as 'the quintessence of the Greatest Name of God'.[68] On the significance of the word to Bahá'ís, Lambden writes:

For Bahá'ís, theologically speaking, the word Bahá as the 'Greatest Name' is a sacred 'word'; a 'mantra' of great magnitude. As the 'Greatest Name', the word Bahá stands at the centre of the Names of God. Indeed, Bahá'u'lláh has stated that all the Divine Names, relative to both the seen and the unseen spheres, are dependent upon it. *The use of the 'Greatest Name' Bahá is thus, in a sense, the alpha and the omega of Bahá'í existence.*[69] [Emphasis mine]

On the significance of the Greatest Name, 'Abdu'l-Bahá said:

> The Greatest Name should be found upon the lips in the first awaking moment of early dawn. It should be fed upon by constant use in daily invocation, in trouble, under opposition, and should be the last word breathed when the head rests upon the pillow at night. It is the name of comfort, protection, happiness, illumination, love and unity.[70]

A Bahá'í zikr or mantra

On the importance of the recitation of the Greatest Name, Bahá'u'lláh said:

> Today, the mantle of deeds and crown of actions is the remembrance of the Most Great Name, both inwardly and outwardly.[71]

The use of the Greatest Name as a Bahá'í 'mantra' is supported by the following words of 'Abdu'l-Bahá:

> Advance always in the Kingdom of Bahá'u'lláh; make always thy heart occupied by the mentioning of Bahá'u'lláh; consider that only in your eyes is Bahá'u'lláh; in your inmost heart is Bahá'u'lláh. If you fall into trouble, say 'Ya-Baha'u'l-Abha'; and if anyone oppose you, say 'Ya-Baha'u'l-Abha'. Even when you may be in your work, mention 'Ya-Baha'u'l-Abha'.[72]

The invocation of the Greatest Name is appropriate for a variety of purposes, from starting and ending the day, to eating meals, to seeking physical and spiritual healing, to asking for guidance and inspiration, and many others.

The Power of the Greatest Name in physical and spiritual healing

Bahá'u'lláh writes,

> Well is it with the physician who cureth ailments in My hallowed and dearly cherished Name.[73]

'Abdu'l-Bahá taught,

> That the Most Great Name exerciseth influence over both physical and spiritual matters is sure and certain.[74]

In another Tablet he writes,

> O maidservant of God! Continue in healing hearts and bodies and seek healing for sick persons by turning unto the Supreme Kingdom and by setting the heart upon obtaining healing through the power of the Greatest Name and by the spirit of the love of God.[75]

The Greatest Name: A shield and protection

> It [The Greatest Name] is the name of comfort, protection. . .[76]

> Burn ye away the veils with the fire of My love, and dispel ye the mists of vain imaginings by the power of this Name through which We have subdued the entire creation.[77]

> Enable him then to seek shelter beneath the shadow of Thy most Exalted Name.[78]

His Name is . . . the supreme talisman.[79]

Today this hallowed Name serveth as a shield for all mankind, and as a veritable refuge for the children of men.[80]

Whenever we were surrounded by calamities, we removed them by the Name of Thy Lord, the Most Exalted the Most Great.[81]

The Greatest Name grants spiritual life and salvation

The use of the Greatest Name and dependence upon it cause the soul to strip itself of the husks of mortality and to step forth free, reborn, a new creature.[82]

Truly, I say unto thee, this blessed Name is the spirit of life, the deliverer from death, the word of salvation and of manifest signs.[83]

His Name is . . . the source of life in both worlds, and of salvation unto such as have gone astray.[84]

The Greatest Name leads to inspiration, guidance, and spiritual perception

Recite the Greatest Name at every morn, and turn thou unto the Kingdom of Abhá, until thou mayest apprehend My mysteries.[85]

The Greatest Name leads to God's grace and confirmations

Call ye to mind the blessed Name of our peerless Beloved, the Abhá Beauty . . . that . . . a fresh outpouring of His grace may stream forth, and a liberal effusion of celestial confirmations may be vouchsafed unto you . . . [86]

Verily, this [The Greatest Name] is the Magnet of divine confirmations. This is the mighty Force which will surely attract heavenly assistance.[87]

I entreat Thee . . . O my God, by Thy Name through which Thou hast guided Thy lovers to the living waters of Thy grace and Thy favours.[88]

The Greatest Name leads to peace of mind, comfort, confidence, strength and glory

Call ye to mind the blessed Name of our peerless Beloved, the Abhá Beauty, in an uplifting spirit of unbounded ecstasy and delight, then unloose your tongues in His praise in such wise that the realm of the heart may be purged from the woes and sorrows of the world of water and clay.[89]

The Greatest Name leads to joy, ecstasy, illumination, love and unity

Let your joy be the joy born of My Most Great Name, a Name that bringeth rapture to the heart, and filleth with ecstasy the minds of all who have drawn nigh unto God.[90]

It is the name of . . . happiness, illumination, love and unity.[91]

The Greatest Name in the morning and evening

The Bahá'í Writings encourage believers to start and end their days with God's Name on their lips:

The Greatest Name should be found upon the lips in the first awakening moment of early dawn. It should be the last word breathed when the head rests upon the pillow at night.[92]

Recite the Greatest Name at every morn.[93]

For example, as you open your eyes in the morning you may wish to say the Greatest Name with a smile on your face. Then, in your mind, hear your soul addressing the Beloved in words such as these, from a prayer revealed by Bahá'u'lláh:

> I have wakened every morning to the light of Thy praise and Thy remembrance.[94]

The Greatest Name to be used at the beginning and end of meals

> When thou wouldst commence eating, start by mentioning My Most Glorious Name (al-abha) and finish it with the Name of Thy Lord, the Possessor of the Throne above and of the earth. [95]

* * *

Likhita Japa or Mantra Writing

A supplementary form of mantra meditation is *likhita japa*[96] or mantra writing. To do likhita japa, write your mantra with full concentration each day in silence, using a special pen and notebook set aside for this purpose.[97] Your mantra should never be far from your heart. When we fall in love with another human being, we want to write their name all over the place. Our mantra or the Name of God should be written in that same spirit. Write His Name as a lover writes the name of their Beloved, with joy and exhilaration.[98]

Mantra writing practice should be another way of seeking God. This entails paying close attention to your writing while you are simultaneously repeating His Name in your mind. On days when calming your mind seems to be a challenge, simply write your mantra in your special notebook as you repeat it mentally. After doing it for a few minutes, your mind will become calm and you can resume your mental repetition in the quiet of your heart.

It is a good idea to decide ahead of time on the number of pages or lines and the time you are going to devote to your mantra writing daily. This will help you become more regular and disciplined in your practice.[99]

12

GRATITUDE MEDITATION

Be thou happy and well pleased and arise to offer thanks to God, in order that thanksgiving may conduce to the increase of bounty.

'Abdu'l-Bahá[1]

To be grateful is being thankful for what we have. It is also an attitude of willingness to receive all the gifts of God that come our way through His grace and bounty. Gratitude is a way of looking at life: when we are grateful, we notice the beauty that is around and within us, we count our blessings even in the midst of a test, for we know that tests are gifts from God and that it is through *them* that we grow spiritually. If we are truly grateful, our glass is half full, not half empty, and we do not wait for all our dreams to be fulfilled before giving ourselves a chance to feel happy. We celebrate each day – no, each moment – as a gift. In practising gratitude, our attitude is one of optimism, faith and trust in God. Therefore, we won't allow worry and fear to rule over us.[2]

In his book *Today We Are Rich*, author and motivational speaker Tim Sanders says:

> Gratefulness will push fear and anxiety out of your consciousness. It's a powerful cleansing agent for your psyche, dissolving any resentment, jealousy, and envy that clog your attitudes with emotional sludge.[3]

Sanders explains the difference between a grateful and an ungrateful person succinctly when he says:

The difference between a grateful person and an ungrateful person lies in perception: One sees a life of beauty; the other sees a life of lack. This explains how someone who is poverty-stricken can find joy in spite of his or her circumstances while many wealthy people can often be miserable in spite of virtually limitless resources.[4]

Many of us have a tendency to take what we already have in life for granted. We see our glass as half empty, not half full! Therefore, we keep living a life of dissatisfaction and dreams that may or may not come true. Instead, if we begin to concentrate on the blessings we already have in life, we can change the way we feel about ourselves and our life, and provide for a more fulfilling and satisfying existence for ourselves and those around us. In his book *Thanks! How the New Science of Gratitude Can Make You Happier*, Robert Emmons shows how research indicates that grateful people experience higher levels of positive emotions such as joy, enthusiasm, love, happiness, and optimism, and that the practice of gratitude as a discipline protects a person from the destructive impulses of envy, resentment, greed or bitterness.[5]

Grateful people consider even little things in life as 'gifts'. For example, having tea with one's family on a Saturday morning, giving our children or spouse a hug, enjoying a picnic on a sunny day, engaging in a heartfelt conversation with a friend, reading a good book, seeing a great movie or theatrical performance, can be viewed as gifts:

> If good things really are better when perceived as gifts, this could be one way that gratitude directly contributes to states of happiness. Grateful people are more likely to perceive things in their lives as sheer gifts and to spontaneously use the language of being 'blessed' and 'gifted by life'.[6]

Gratitude is a trait we need to take time to cultivate in ourselves and in our children. If we want to have grateful children, we need to develop the practice of gratitude in them from an early age, because it takes effort and perseverance to become grateful.

> Ingratitude is natural – like weeds. Gratitude is like a rose. It has
> to be fed and watered and cultivated and loved and protected.[7]

Gratefulness as well as other positive emotions can also influence our pain perception. Studies conducted by Sheldon Cohen, the Carnegie-Mellon health psychologist, indicate that positive emotions (such as gratitude) may have analgesic effects stimulating the release of the brain's own morphinelike substances.[8]

As we begin to look for things in our lives to be grateful for and gradually cultivate an attitude of gratitude within ourselves, we begin to appreciate simple pleasures and things that we used to take for granted. We not only notice the little 'gifts' that come our way but also look for the good, even in undesirable situations.

Here are some ways to cultivate the attitude of gratitude in our lives:

Visual reminders. Emmons suggests using visual reminders such as magnets with inspiring quotations on gratitude, at our home or our workplace as a tool to develop the attitude of gratitude.

Keeping a gratitude journal. Emmons also encourages us to keep a 'gratitude journal' to keep a daily record of our blessings. This practice will add to our happiness:

> When we are grateful, we affirm that a source of goodness exists
> in our lives. By writing each day, we magnify and expand upon
> these sources of goodness. Setting aside time on a daily basis
> to recall moments of gratitude associated with even mundane
> or ordinary events, your personal attributes, or valued people
> in your life gives you the potential to interweave and thread
> together a sustainable life theme of gratefulness.[9]

The concept of a gratitude journal was made famous by Sarah Ban Breathnach's book *The Simple Abundance: Journal of Gratitude.*

One way of carrying out this exercise is to list at least five things for which we are grateful, at the end of each day. They can consist of things that happened during the day which added to the happiness of our day, or just the people, things, qualities, and opportunities we have in our lives for which we are grateful. As we list these items, it would be helpful to refer to them as 'gifts'. For instance, I am grateful to God for the gift of faith, the gift of my loving family, or the gift of the opportunity of service which brings so much joy to my heart.

Gratitude moment. We can begin to look for finding joy even in the small things that happen to us daily – things that we ordinarily take for granted. A gratitude moment can consist of enjoying a warm cup of tea on a cold day, listening to a soothing piece of music that elevates our soul, or even enjoying the beauty and scent of hyacinths in the spring. As the American writer Jean Webster (1876–1916) said: 'It isn't the big pleasures that count the most; it is making a great deal out of the little ones.'

Wearing a 'gratitude wristband'. This may help us to be constantly aware of the things in life for which we are grateful.

Imagining losing what we have in life. This is a very powerful way of reminding ourselves to be more appreciative of the blessings of God in our lives and in ourselves.

A gratitude card or a gratitude letter. When you've been at a shop and a salesperson goes out of his or her way to assist you, you may want to send them a note expressing your appreciation for what they have done. By doing so, you not only feel wonderful for doing what is right, you will help cultivate the quality of kindness in them. Another way to do this is to simply call the management of the store to inform them of the fine job that particular employee is doing. In this way, he or she may even be rewarded financially for doing a great job as well. Some large supermarkets now make it easy to do this by filling out a card instore.

Example of an indoor meditation area. This one is the author's meditation room, showing the 'inner child' photographs.

A treasure chest

Example of Likhita Japa writing (Arabic) from the author's notebook

Example of Likhita Japa writing (English) from the author's notebook

The Ascent of the Blessed (Ascent into the Empyrean), Hieronymus Bosch (c. 1500), with permission of the Palazzo Ducale, Venice.

Example of an image for visualization:
The Land of the Beloved,
photo courtesy of http: www.thinkstockphotos.co.uk.

Example of an image for visualization: The Land of the Beloved,
photo courtesy of Olivyaz Blogspot: http://olivyaz.blogspot.com/2010_01_01_archive.html

Example of an image for visualization: A Pond of Serenity, photo courtesy of http: www.thinkstockphotos.co.uk.

Example of image for waterfall and light visualization, photo courtesy of
http://www.wallconvert.com/converted/windows-7--10_wallpapers_14848_1920x1200-16625.html

Weekly gratitude session. Once a week the family can come together for a 'gratitude session'. The meeting can start with a prayer and contemplation on some scriptural passages about the virtue of gratitude. Then, each member of the group can list the things that happened to them in the course of the past week for which they are grateful. If they cannot think of any new events, they can always be reminded to be thankful for the people or things in their lives. This can be an effective way of cultivating gratitude in ourselves and our children.

Practising Gratitude Meditation

Sit in your sacred space or any other place where you can have peace and quiet. Close your eyes. Visualize yourself surrounded by the warmth of the Light of God's love and presence and as you smile, begin your meditation by reaching out to Him mentally through your mantra. As you continue to feel His loving presence, spend the next 5–10 minutes reflecting on all the blessings in your life. This can include the blessing of having God's love in your heart, your spiritual values and traits, your health, your family and friends, your work, your possessions, and the opportunities you have had to serve others. One by one, bring them to mind and as you do so, thank God for each of these blessings. Remember that when you give thanks, sadness finds no room to grow in your mind and heart. Giving thanks helps your spiritual side grow gradually and, over time, become the dominant side of your personality.

In *Memorials of the Faithful,* 'Abdu'l-Bahá gives the inspiring story of Muḥammad-'Alí of Isfahan, who demonstrated thankfulness for even the smallest things in life:

> . . . he had little to live on, but was happy and content . . . He spent his days in utter bliss . . . he carried on a small business, which occupied him from morning till noon. In the afternoons he would take his samovar,[10] wrap it in a dark-coloured pouch made from a saddle-bag, and go off somewhere to a garden or meadow, or out in a field, and have his tea . . .

Muḥammad-'Alí would carefully consider every blessing that came his way. 'How delicious my tea is today,' he would comment. 'What perfume, what colour! How lovely this meadow is, and the flowers so bright!' He used to say that everything, even air and water, had its own special fragrance. For him the days passed in indescribable delight. Even kings were not so happy as this old man, the people said. 'He is completely free of the world,' they would declare: 'He lives in joy.'[11]

In numerous passages from their sacred Writings, Bahá'ís are encouraged to cultivate the virtue of gratitude:

Ponder ye in your hearts the grace and the blessings of God and render thanks unto Him at eventide and at dawn.[12]

The essence of charity is for the servant to recount the blessings of his Lord, and to render thanks unto Him at all times and under all conditions.[13]

The truth is that God has endowed man with virtues, powers and ideal faculties of which nature is entirely bereft and by which man is elevated, distinguished and superior. We must thank God for these bestowals, for these powers He has given us, for this crown He has placed upon our heads.[14]

They can also offer gratitude prayers such as this one:

He is God, exalted is He, the Lord of might and grandeur!
O God, my God! I yield Thee thanks at all times and render Thee praise under all conditions.

In prosperity, all praise is Thine, O Lord of the Worlds, and in its absence, all gratitude is Thine, O Desire of them that have recognized Thee!

In adversity, all honour is Thine, O Adored One of all who are in heaven and on earth, and in affliction, all glory is Thine, O Enchanter of the hearts of those who yearn after Thee!

In hardship, all praise is Thine, O Thou the Goal of them that seek after Thee, and in comfort, all thanksgiving is Thine, O Thou whose remembrance is treasured in the hearts of those who are nigh unto Thee!

In wealth, all splendour is Thine, O Lord of them that are devoted to Thee, and in poverty, all command is Thine, O Thou the Hope of them that acknowledge Thy unity!

In joy, all glory is Thine, O Thou besides Whom there is none other God, and in sorrow, all beauty is Thine, O Thou besides Whom there is none other God!

In hunger, all justice is Thine, O Thou besides Whom there is none other God, and in satiety, all grace is Thine, O Thou besides Whom there is none other God!

In my homeland, all bounty is Thine, O Thou besides Whom there is none other God, and in exile, all decree is Thine, O Thou besides Whom there is none other God!

Under the sword, all munificence is Thine, O Thou besides Whom there is none other God, and in the safety of home, all perfection is Thine, O Thou besides Whom there is none other God!

In the lofty mansion, all generosity is Thine, O Thou besides Whom there is none other God, and upon the lowly dust, all favour is Thine, O Thou besides Whom there is none other God!

In prison, all fidelity is Thine, O Thou the Bestower of gifts, and in confinement, all eternity is Thine, O Thou Who art the ever-abiding King!

All bounty is Thine, O Thou Who art the Lord of bounty, and the Sovereign of bounty, and the King of bounty! I bear witness that Thou art to be praised in Thy doings, O Thou Source of bounty, and to be obeyed in Thy behests, O Thou ocean of bounty, He from Whom all bounty doth proceed He to Whom all bounty doth return![15]

Followers of other great religions of the world have also been encouraged to practise the quality of gratefulness:

O you who have attained to faith! Partake of the good things which We have provided for you as sustenance, and render thanks unto God, if it is [truly] Him that you worship.[16]

The unworthy man is ungrateful, forgetful of benefits [done to him]. This ingratitude, this forgetfulness is congenial to mean people . . . But the worthy person is grateful and mindful of benefits done to him. This gratitude, this mindfulness, is congenial to the best people.[17]

It is God who has made the night for you, so that you might rest therein, and the day, to make [you] see. Behold, God is indeed limitless in His bounty unto man – but most men are ungrateful . . . It is God who has made the earth a resting place for you and the sky a canopy, and has formed you – and formed you so well – and provided for you sustenance out of the good things of life. Such is God, your Sustainer; hallowed, then, is God, the Sustainer of all the worlds![18]

13

MUSIC MEDITATION

Music is one of the important arts. It has a great effect upon the human spirit.

'Abdu'l-Bahá[1]

In the Bahá'í Faith music is viewed as a ladder through which our souls can ascend to the higher realm:

> We, verily, have made music as a ladder for your souls, a means whereby they may be lifted up unto the realm on high . . .[2]

Music is also regarded as the spiritual food for our hearts and souls. In this regard, 'Abdu'l-Bahá says:

> The art of music is divine and effective. It is the food of the soul and spirit. Through the power and charm of music the spirit of man is uplifted.[3]

And again:

> The musician's art is among those arts worthy of the highest praise, and it moveth the hearts of all who grieve.[4]

Although music or an ordinary pleasing voice is of the physical realm, yet it has an effect upon the spirit. In the same manner, freshness and purity of the air, the atmosphere, the scenery and sweet fragrances impart joy, spirituality and comfort to the heart. Even though these are physical phenomena they have a great spiritual influence.[5]

To Mary L. Lucas, who was on pilgrimage to 'Akká, 'Abdu'l-Bahá said that music can awaken our individual essence:

> Music really awakens the real, natural nature, the individual essence. With whatever purpose you listen to music, that purpose will be increased.[6]

Practising Music Meditation

Sit in a quiet place, close your eyes, and take a few breaths. Next, play a soothing piece of music of your choice. Become totally absorbed in the music you are listening to. Do your best to stay in the present. When thoughts appear, let them pass by like birds in the sky, and gently bring your mind back to the music as you enjoy it with every fibre of your being. This meditation will not only bring you peace of mind, it is a good practice for training the mind to be focused.

14

CONTEMPLATION OR REFLECTION ON THE WORD OF GOD

Meditate upon that which hath streamed forth from the heaven of the Will of Thy Lord, He Who is the Source of all grace, that thou mayest grasp the intended meaning which is enshrined in the sacred depths of the Holy Writings.

Bahá'u'lláh[1]

Another advantage of meditation is its potential for transforming us into highly spiritual beings who seek closeness to God. Imagine the heart and mind as gardens which, instead of flowers, have grown weeds and thorns. Now visualize negative qualities such as anger, hatred, greed, envy or worry as these weeds and thorns. Over time, disciplined meditation can help us gradually remove these. We can then grow roses and other beautiful flowers in their place. Daily contemplation and reflection can serve as regular watering, so that the beautiful rose-garden of your heart and mind remains fresh and fragrant. This is a mighty task which requires much patience, devotion and steadfastness, but the reward is invaluable. On the subject of reading the Word of God and discovering its gems, Bahá'u'lláh writes:

Immerse yourselves in the ocean of My words, that ye may unravel its secrets, and discover all the pearls of wisdom that lie hid in its depths.[2]

And further:

> Do thou meditate on that which We have revealed unto thee,
> that thou mayest discover the purpose of God, thy Lord, and
> the Lord of all worlds. In these words the mysteries of Divine
> Wisdom have been treasured.[3]

Contemplation on the Word of God gradually leads to spiritual
transformation:

> Is it within human power, O Ḥakím,[4] to effect in the constitu-
> ent elements of any of the minute and indivisible particles of
> matter so complete a transformation as to transmute it into
> purest gold? Perplexing and difficult as this may appear, the
> still greater task of converting satanic strength into heavenly
> power is one that We have been empowered to accomplish.
> The Force capable of such a transformation transcendeth the
> potency of the Elixir itself. The Word of God, alone, can claim
> the distinction of being endowed with the capacity required
> for so great and far-reaching a change.[5]

Again He writes:

> Every word that proceedeth out of the mouth of God is
> endowed with such potency as can instill new life into every
> human frame.[6]

Reflection on the Word of God awakens us to our true nature and
guides us to the straight Path. The following verses are cited in
support of these ideas:

> Every verse which this pen hath revealed is a bright and shining
> portal that discloseth the glories of a saintly and pious life, of
> pure and stainless deeds.[7]

By contemplating the Word of God, we learn to be submissive to

His Will and abide by His laws which are a mighty stronghold for our protection. Bahá'u'lláh writes:

> Were any man to ponder in his heart that which the Pen of the Most High hath revealed and to taste of its sweetness, he would, of a certainty, find himself emptied and delivered from his own desires, and utterly subservient to the Will of the Almighty. Happy is the man that hath attained so high a station, and hath not deprived himself of so bountiful a grace.[8]

This has been a recurrent theme in religion, for instance in this verse from the Old Testament:

> This book of the law shall not depart out of your mouth, but you shall meditate on it day and night, that you may be careful to do according to all that is written in it; for then you shall make your way prosperous, and then you shall have good success.[9]

Among the many fruits of contemplation on the Word of God are a change in our character, peace of mind and spiritual elation:

> Peace of mind is gained by the centering of the spiritual consciousness on the Prophet of God; therefore you should study the spiritual Teachings, and receive the Water of Life from the Holy Utterances. Then by translating these high ideals into action, your entire character will be changed, and your mind will not only find peace, but your entire being will find joy and enthusiasm.[10]

> The heavenly teachings are expressed in parable in order to be understood and preserved for ages to come. When the spiritually minded dive deeply into the ocean of their meaning they bring to the surface the pearls of their inner significance. There is no greater pleasure than to study God's Word with a spiritual mind.[11]

Reflecting on the Word of God and planting its meaning in our heart and mind is conducive to the love of God, which is the primary purpose for our creation:

> . . . every breast which committeth His Words to memory, God shall cause, if it were that of a believer, to be filled with His love . . .[12]

Evening and Morning Contemplation

Daily contemplation on the Word of God is indispensable in our journey from our self to God. It is through reflection and contemplation on His Word that our souls find spiritual nourishment. In the Bahá'í Faith, Bahá'u'lláh enjoins His followers to recite the verses of God in the morning and in the evening:

> Recite ye the verses of God every morning and eventide. Whoso faileth to recite them hath not been faithful to the Covenant of God and His Testament, and whoso turneth away from these holy verses in this Day is of those who throughout eternity have turned away from God. Fear ye God, O My servants, one and all.[13]

One of the great sources of spiritual nourishment in the Bahá'í Faith is Bahá'u'lláh's Hidden Words, a mystical work that focuses on the relationship between the Creator and humanity:

> Read ye The Hidden Words, ponder the inner meanings, act in accord therewith . . . and rise up as ye are bidden in the heavenly teachings.[14]

One day in 1912 the beloved Master was very stern while in New York. He held the book of Hidden Words in His hand and walked back and forth and then lifted the book high and said, 'Whoever does not live up to these Words, is not of Me.'[15]

'Abdu'l-Bahá is also reported to have said:

> . . . investigate and study the Holy Scriptures word by word so
> that you may attain knowledge of the mysteries hidden therein.
> Be not satisfied with words, but seek to understand the spir-
> itual meanings hidden in the heart of the words . . . These are
> the mysteries of God. It is not the reading of the words that
> profits you; it is the understanding of their meanings. There-
> fore, pray God that you may be enabled to comprehend the
> mysteries of the divine Testaments . . .
>
> All the texts and teachings of the holy Testaments have
> intrinsic spiritual meanings. They are not to be taken literally
> . . . May your souls be illumined by the light of the Words of
> God, and may you become repositories of the mysteries of
> God, for no comfort is greater and no happiness is sweeter
> than spiritual comprehension of the divine teachings.[16]

A Suggested Approach to Daily Contemplation

In the morning, before you start reading the passage you have
selected, turn to God and thank Him for the 'gift' of His Word
that is the source of guidance and spiritual transformation in your
life. Next, ask for His assistance in enlightening your mind with
understanding of the verses you are about to recite. Then, read
the verses a couple of times and spend a few minutes in reflection
and contemplation. Next, close your eyes and think about what
God is telling you through the words you have read. What does
the passage mean to you? How can it be implemented in your life?
Then, ask for His grace and confirmation to live accordingly.[17]

Imagine the meaning of the passage as a beautiful flower and
plant it in your heart as you would plant a flower in a garden.
Repeat it throughout the day as time allows. You can even write
the passage on a piece of paper and have it with you throughout
the day as a source of spiritual nourishment. In the evening, refer
to the same passage or choose another quotation for your end of
the day reflection and contemplation.

Daily Accountability

> O Son of Being! Bring thyself to account each day ere thou art summoned to a reckoning; for death, unheralded, shall come upon thee and thou shalt be called to give account for thy deeds.[18]

A complementary practice to meditation is the 'daily accountability' exercise, which can be done at the end of the day through self-examination with the intent of spiritual growth – that is, to become more patient, more compassionate, more polite, more honest, more just, more loving, and so on. It is through the reflection of such heavenly qualities that are latent within our souls that we can be *truly* happy. After all, aren't we created in the 'image of God'?

> Man is, in reality, a spiritual being, and only when he lives in the spirit is he truly happy.[19]

> . . . every one must consider at the end of each day what have been his actions. If he finds something which would please God, he must thank Him and pray to be strengthened to do this good act throughout his life; but if his actions have not been approvable or honest, he must earnestly ask God for strength to do better.[20]

To carry out our daily accountability exercise, we can sit in our meditation place and take a few breaths to calm our minds. Then we can start by reviewing our day from the time we got up. We don't have to recall *everything* we have done; the major events and experiences will be enough. As we remember each event, we can simply reflect on it to see if we can learn anything from each experience.

The aim here, as Roger Walsh writes, is 'to learn, not to blame; to grow in wisdom, not to fall into guilt; to appreciate our strength as much as to recognize our weaknesses . . . Regular self-reflection fosters good choices.'[21]

Spiritual transformation, which is the ultimate goal for our earthly existence according to the divine religions, is a process that will take us a lifetime. One of the most effective approaches to our spiritual transformation is the practice of daily accountability.

Bahá'u'lláh writes:

> Let each morn be better than its eve and each morrow richer than its yesterday. [22]

A similar injunction can be seen in the following statement of the Buddha:

> Let a wise man remove impurities from himself even as a silversmith removes impurities from the silver; one after one, little by little, again and again. [23]

Other Ideas for Contemplation

Garden of Delight

During my daily contemplation on excerpts or passages from the sacred scriptures of different religions, I have come across many beautiful verses which moved me. I began to collect these 'spiritual gems' in exquisite notebooks. Over time, I collected many such notebooks and decided to keep them in a 'treasure chest' (see photograph section) which I placed in a corner of our meditation room. I would also hand-pick those that I felt were especially powerful and needed to see daily, and taped those to the cabinet doors and the wall in a corner of my kitchen area. This is an area I pass by frequently during the day. In addition, by posting selected passages in the kitchen area, the whole family gets a chance to benefit from the wisdom and love enshrined in them. Even guests have stopped by this Garden of Delight and fed and nourished their souls with its fruits.

THE DIVINE ART OF MEDITATION

Creating an evening oasis

> . . . husband and wife should be united both physically and spiritually, that they may ever improve the spiritual life of each other, and may enjoy everlasting unity throughout all the worlds of God.[24]

> Strive . . . to abide, heart and soul, with each other as two doves in the nest, for this is to be blessed in both worlds.[25]

I believe that even though physical and intellectual attraction are important in a marriage, it is spiritual attraction that is most important and can be the key ingredient for sustaining couples through tests and trials in their spiritual journey here on earth. Ideally, the couple would be spiritually attracted to each other before the marriage, based on shared values. Then, after the marriage, the spouses can nurture and reinforce their spiritual bonding through other means, including joint meditative exercises. One such method is what I call an *evening oasis.* This is a simple practice that not only leads to peace of mind for the couple, but will also enable them to connect with one another on a deeper level.

To enjoy your evening oasis, go to a quiet place in your home, preferably your meditation room (or meditation corner). Then take a few deep breaths to relax your mind and body. Begin by playing some calming music and reading selected passages from various Holy Scriptures. You may wish to choose from the verses provided in Chapter 15 of this book. As you read each verse together, try to reflect on the underlying message of the text and see how you can apply it to your life as a couple. Share your understanding of the verse with each other. Then, if you have internet access, look for a relaxation video and watch it together. You can find a huge selection of such videos on YouTube, for example. You can bookmark these videos or even create a playlist of them on YouTube. Relaxation videos often have soothing background music and beautiful scenery. They can be of tremendous help in achieving peace of mind and can even help you fall sleep faster.

Ideally, you want to engage in the evening oasis every evening you are together. If you can't do this, then do it as often as possible. Consistency is the key.

Collecting 'Pearls of Wisdom'

Notebook

As you immerse yourselves in the study of the world's sacred literature, you can pick and choose the passages that touch your heart the most or those that speak to your heart. Collect them in a notebook as 'pearls of wisdom' and refer to them regularly. If you end up with too many such notebooks, put them in a treasure box, as previously described. You can even try to commit some of the shorter passages to memory. They may prove particularly helpful in times of tests and uncertainty in your life.

Making bookmarks

An approach that will help you keep your contact with the soul-refreshing Word of God is to make bookmarks with these 'pearls of wisdom'. You may be able to find bookmarks with holy scriptural verses, but they may not be the ones you feel *your* soul needs to be nourished with on a regular basis.

Sharing spiritual food with family and friends

If you see interest in meditation or spirituality in your inner circle of friends or family, you can share your 'pearls of wisdom' with them as well. Consider this an act of service to help nourish their souls. Either e-mail them select passages every so often, or print some of the best ones on nice stationery so they can be framed and put up on a wall. Alternatively, your family and friends might like to take the passages to work in their purse or briefcase and draw strength and wisdom from them in moments of need.

15

PASSAGES FOR CONTEMPLATION

Happy are they who, with the waters of divine utterance, have cleansed their hearts from all allusions, whisperings and suggestions, and who have fixed their gaze upon the Dayspring of Glory.

Bahá'u'lláh[1]

This chapter consists of some passages from the sacred scriptures of the world that I have found helpful in reflecting on the Word of God.

The Bhagavad Gita

Offer to me all thy works and rest thy mind on the Supreme. Be free from vain hopes and selfish thoughts, and with inner peace fight thou thy fight . . . Hate and lust for things of nature have their roots in man's lower nature. Let him not fall under their power; they are the two enemies in his path.[2]

. . . let thy aim be the good of all, and then carry on thy task in life.[3]

The path that a great man follows becomes a guide to the world.[4]

. . . he who loves me shall not perish.[5]

The man who has a good will for all, who is friendly and has compassion; who has no thoughts of 'I' or 'mine', whose peace is the same in pleasures and sorrows, and who is forgiving; . . . whose determination is strong; whose mind and inner vision are set on me-this man loves me, and he is dear to me.[6]

He whose peace is not shaken by others, and before whom other people find peace, beyond excitement and anger and fear – he is dear to me.

He who is free from vain expectations, who is pure, who is wise and knows what to do, who in inner peace watches both sides, who shakes not, who works for God and not for himself – this man loves me, and he is dear to me. He who feels neither excitement nor repulsion, who complains not and lusts not for things; who is beyond good and evil, and who has love – he is dear to me.

The man whose love is the same for his enemies or his friends, whose soul is the same in honour or disgrace . . . Who is balanced in blame and in praise, whose soul is silent, who is happy with whatever he has, whose home is not in this world, and who has love – this man is dear to me.

But even dearer to me are those who have faith and love, and who have me as their End Supreme: those who hear my words of Truth, and who come to the waters of Everlasting Life.[7]

The Dhammapada

What we are today comes from our thoughts of yesterday, and our present thoughts build our life of tomorrow; our life is the creation of our mind. If a man speaks or acts with an impure mind, suffering follows him as the wheel of the cart follows the beast that draws the cart.[8]

'He insulted me, he hurt me, he defeated me, he robbed me.' Those who think such thoughts will not be free from hate . . .

For hate is not conquered by hate; hate is conquered by love. This is the law eternal. Many do not know that we are here in this world to live in harmony. Those who know this do not fight against each other. He who lives only for pleasures, and whose soul is not in harmony, who considers not the food he eats, is idle and has not the power of virtue – such a man is moved by Mara, is moved by selfish temptations, even as a weak tree is shaken by the wind. But he who lives not for pleasures, and whose soul is in self-harmony, who eats or fasts with moderation, and has faith and the power of virtue – this man is not moved by temptations, as a great rock is not shaken by the wind.[9]

Find joy in watchfulness; guard well your mind. Uplift yourself from your lower self, even as an elephant draws himself out of a muddy swamp.[10]

Make an island for yourself. Hasten and strive. Be wise. With the dust of impurities blown off, and free from sinful passions, you will come unto the glorious land of the great.[11]

Just as a man who has long been far away is welcomed with joy on his safe return by his relatives, well-wishers and friends; in the same way the good works of a man in his life welcome him in another life, with the joy of a friend meeting a friend on his return.[12]

The glorious chariots of kings wear out, and the body wears out and grows old; but the virtue of the good never grows old, and thus they can teach the good to those who are good.[13]

Hold not a deed of little worth, thinking 'this is little to me'. The falling of drops of water will in time fill a water-jar. Even so the wise man becomes full of good, although he gather it little by little.[14]

For he whose mind is well trained in the ways that lead to light, who surrenders the bondage of attachments and finds joy in his freedom from bondage, who free from the darkness of passions shines pure in a radiance of light, even in this mortal life he enjoys the immortal Nirvana. [15]

These are my sons. This is my wealth. In this way the fool troubles himself. He is not even the owner of himself: how much less of his sons and of his wealth! [16]

As from a large heap of flowers many garlands and wreaths can be made, so by a mortal in this life there is much good work to be done. [17]

The Bible

Hear, O Israel: The Lord our God is one Lord; and you shall love the Lord your God with all your heart, and with all your soul, and with all your might. And these words which I command you this day shall be upon your heart; and you shall teach them diligently to your children, and shall talk of them when you sit in your house, and when you walk by the way, and when you lie down, and when you rise. [18]

Blessed is the man who walks not in the counsel of the wicked, nor stands in the way of sinners, nor sits in the seat of scoffers; but his delight is in the law of the Lord, and on his law he meditates day and night. He is like a tree planted by streams of water, that yields its fruit in its season, and its leaf does not wither. In all that he does, he prospers. [19]

The Lord is my rock, and my fortress, and my deliverer, my God, my rock, in whom I take refuge . . . [20]

Wait for the Lord; be strong, and let your heart take courage. [21]

The Lord is my light and my salvation, whom shall I fear? The Lord is the stronghold of my life; of whom shall I be afraid?[22]

One thing have I asked of the Lord, that I will seek after; that I may dwell in the house of the Lord all the days of my life, to behold the beauty of the Lord. [23]

His [God] praise shall continually be in my mouth.[24]

Happy is the man who takes refuge in Him.[25]

Many are the afflictions of the righteous; but the Lord delivers him out of them all.[26]

. . . man heaps up, and knows not who will gather![27]

Whom have I in heaven but thee? And there is nothing upon earth that I desire besides thee. My flesh and my heart may fail, but God is the strength of my heart and my portion for ever.[28]

Because he cleaves to me in love, I will deliver him; I will protect him, because he knows my name. When he calls to me, I will answer him; I will be with him in trouble.[29]

I love those who love me, and those who seek me diligently find me.[30]

Do not boast about tomorrow, for you do not know what a day may bring forth. Let another praise you, and not your own mouth; a stranger, and not your own lips.[31]

. . . he who trusts in the Lord is safe.[32]

Blessed are the poor in spirit, for theirs is the kingdom of heaven.

Blessed are those who mourn, for they shall be comforted.

Blessed are the meek, for they shall inherit the earth.

Blessed are those who hunger and thirst for righteousness, for they shall be satisfied.

Blessed are the merciful, for they shall obtain mercy.

Blessed are the pure in heart, for they shall see God.

Blessed are the peacemakers, for they shall be called sons of God.

Blessed are those who are persecuted for righteousness' sake, for theirs is the kingdom of heaven.

Blessed are you when men revile you and persecute you and utter all kinds of evil against you falsely on my account. Rejoice and be glad, for your reward is great in heaven, for so men persecuted the prophets who were before you.

You are the salt of the earth; but if salt has lost its taste, how shall its saltness be restored? It is no longer good for anything except to be thrown out and trodden under foot by men.[33]

Do not lay up for yourselves treasures on earth, where moth and rust consume and where thieves break in and steal, but lay up for yourselves treasures in heaven, where neither moth nor rust consumes and where thieves do not break in and steal. For where your treasure is, there will your heart also be.[34]

Judge not, that you be not judged.[35]

Why do you see the speck that is in your brother's eye, but do not notice the log that is in your own eye? Or how can you say to your brother, 'Let me take the speck out of your eye' when there is the log in your own eye?[36]

Ask and it will be given to you; seek and you will find; knock, and it will be opened to you. For every one who asks receives, and he who seeks finds, and to him who knocks, it will be opened.[37]

You have heard that it was said, 'An eye for an eye and a tooth for a tooth.' But I say to you, Do not resist one who is evil. But if any one strikes you on the right cheek, turn to him the other also; . . . You have heard that it was said, 'You shall love your neighbor and hate your enemy.' But I say to you, Love your enemies and pray for those who persecute you, so that you may be sons of your Father who is in heaven; . . . For if you love those who love you, what reward have you?[38]

And let us not grow weary in well-doing, for in due season we shall reap, if we do not lose heart.[39]

Be patient toward all men.[40]

The Qur'án

True piety does not consist in turning your faces towards the east or the west – but truly pious is he who believes in God, and the Last Day, and the angels, and revelation, and the prophets; and spends his substance – however much he himself may cherish it – upon his near of kin, and the orphans, and the needy, and the wayfarer, and the beggars, and for the freeing of human beings from bondage; and is constant in prayer, and renders the purifying dues; and [truly pious are] they who keep their promises whenever they promise, and are patient in misfortune and hardship and in time of peril; it is they that have proved themselves true, and it is they, they who are conscious of God.[41]

And be constant in prayer, and render the purifying dues; for, whatever good deed you send ahead for your own selves, you shall find it with God; behold, God sees all that you do.[42]

And if My servants ask thee about Me – behold, I am near; I respond to the call of him who calls, whenever he calls unto Me: let them, then, respond unto Me, and believe in Me, so that they might follow the right way.[43]

God loves those who are patient in adversity.[44]

Say: 'Behold, my prayer, and [all] my acts of worship, and my living and my dying are for God [alone], the Sustainer of all the worlds.[45]

Verily, that which is with God is by far the best for you, if you but knew it; all that is with you is bound to come to an end, whereas that which is with God is everlasting.[46]

. . . neither allow yourselves to speak ill of one another behind your backs. Would any of you like to eat the flesh of his dead brother? Nay, you would loathe it![47]

Now, verily, it is We who have created man, and We know what his innermost self whispers within him; for We are closer to him than his neck-vein.[48]

God does not burden any human being with more than He has given him – [and it may well be that] God will grant, after hardship, ease.[49]

And unto everyone who is conscious of God, He [always] grants a way out [of unhappiness]. And provides for him in a manner beyond all expectation; and for everyone who places his trust in God, He [alone] is enough.[50]

And behold, with every hardship comes ease; verily, with every hardship comes ease![51]

The Bahá'í Faith

O My Brother! A pure heart is as a mirror; cleanse it with the burnish of love and severance from all save God, that the true sun may shine within it and the eternal morning dawn. Then wilt thou clearly see the meaning of 'Neither doth My earth nor My heaven contain Me, but the heart of My faithful servant containeth Me.' And thou wilt take up thy life in thine hand, and with infinite longing cast it before the new Beloved One.[52]

Be generous in prosperity, and thankful in adversity. Be worthy of the trust of thy neighbour, and look upon him with a bright and friendly face. Be a treasure to the poor, an admonisher to the rich, an answerer of the cry of the needy, a preserver of the sanctity of thy pledge. Be fair in thy judgement, and guarded in thy speech. Be unjust to no man, and show all meekness to all men. Be as a lamp unto them that walk in darkness, a joy to the sorrowful, a sea for the thirsty, a haven for the distressed, an upholder and defender of the victim of oppression. Let integrity and uprightness distinguish all thine acts. Be a home for the stranger, a balm to the suffering, a tower of strength for the fugitive. Be eyes to the blind, and a guiding light unto the feet of the erring. Be an ornament to the countenance of truth, a crown to the brow of fidelity, a pillar of the temple of righteousness, a breath of life to the body of mankind, an ensign of the hosts of justice, a luminary above the horizon of virtue, a dew to the soil of the human heart, an ark on the ocean of knowledge, a sun in the heaven of bounty, a gem on the diadem of wisdom, a shining light in the firmament of thy generation, a fruit upon the tree of humility.[53]

Summon ye, then, the people to God, and invite humanity to follow the example of the Company on high. Be ye loving fathers to the orphan, and a refuge to the helpless, and a treasury for the poor, and a cure for the ailing. Be ye the helpers of every victim of oppression, the patrons of the disadvantaged. Think ye at all times of rendering some service to every member of the human race. Pay ye no heed to aversion and rejection, to disdain, hostility, injustice: act ye in the opposite way. Be ye sincerely kind, not in appearance only. Let each one of God's loved ones centre his attention on this: to be the Lord's mercy to man; to be the Lord's grace. Let him do some good to every person whose path he crosseth, and be of some benefit to him. Let him improve the character of each and all, and reorient the minds of men. In this way, the light of divine guidance will shine forth, and the blessings of God will cradle all mankind: for love is light, no matter in what abode it dwelleth; and hate is darkness, no matter where it may make its nest.[54]

O My servants! Could ye apprehend with what wonders of My munificence and bounty I have willed to entrust your souls, ye would, of a truth, rid yourselves of attachment to all created things, and would gain a true knowledge of your own selves – a knowledge which is the same as the comprehension of Mine own Being. Ye would find yourselves independent of all else but Me, and would perceive, with your inner and outer eye, and as manifest as the revelation of My effulgent Name, the seas of My loving-kindness and bounty moving within you. Suffer not your idle fancies, your evil passions, your insincerity and blindness of heart to dim the lustre, or stain the sanctity, of so lofty a station. Ye are even as the bird which soareth, with the full force of its mighty wings and with complete and joyous confidence, through the immensity of the heavens, until, impelled to satisfy its hunger, it turneth longingly to the water and clay of the earth below it, and, having been entrapped in the mesh of its desire, findeth itself impotent to resume its flight to the realms whence it came. Powerless to shake off the burden weighing on its sullied wings, that bird, hitherto an inmate of the heavens, is now forced to seek a dwelling-place upon the dust. Wherefore, O My servants, defile not your wings with the clay of waywardness and vain desires, and suffer them not to be stained with the dust of envy and hate, that ye may not be hindered from soaring in the heavens of My divine knowledge.

. . . The world is but a show, vain and empty, a mere nothing, bearing the semblance of reality. Set not your affections upon it. Break not the bond that uniteth you with your Creator, and be not of those that have erred and strayed from His ways. Verily I say, the world is like the vapour in a desert, which the thirsty dreameth to be water and striveth after it with all his might, until when he cometh unto it, he findeth it to be mere illusion. It may, moreover, be likened unto the lifeless image of the beloved whom the lover hath sought and found, in the end, after long search and to his utmost regret, to be such as cannot 'fatten nor appease his hunger'.

O My servants! Sorrow not if, in these days and on this earthly plane, things contrary to your wishes have been ordained and manifested by God, for days of blissful joy, of heavenly delight, are assuredly in store for you. Worlds, holy and spiritually glorious, will be unveiled to your eyes. You are destined by Him, in this world and hereafter, to partake of their benefits, to share in their joys, and to obtain a portion of their sustaining grace. To each and every one of them you will, no doubt, attain.[55]

There can be no doubt whatever that, in consequence of the efforts which every man may consciously exert and as a result of the exertion of his own spiritual faculties, this mirror can be so cleansed from the dross of earthly defilements and purged from satanic fancies as to be able to draw nigh unto the meads of eternal holiness and attain the courts of everlasting fellowship.[56]

. . . nearness to God is possible through devotion to Him, through entrance into the Kingdom and service to humanity; it is attained by unity with mankind and through loving-kindness to all; it is dependent upon investigation of truth, acquisition of praiseworthy virtues, service in the cause of universal peace and personal sanctification. In a word, nearness to God necessitates sacrifice of self, severance and the giving up of all to Him. Nearness is likeness.[57]

If his [man's] morals become spiritual in character, his aspirations heavenly and his actions conformable to the will of God, man has attained the image and likeness of his Creator . . . [58]

That one indeed is a man who, today, dedicateth himself to the service of the entire human race. The Great Being saith: Blessed and happy is he that ariseth to promote the best interests of the peoples and kindreds of the earth. In another passage He hath proclaimed: It is not for him to pride himself who loveth his own country, but rather for him who loveth the whole world. The earth is but one country, and mankind its citizens. [59]

Is it not astonishing that although man has been created for the knowledge and love of God, for the virtues of the human world, for spirituality, heavenly illumination and eternal life, nevertheless, he continues ignorant and negligent of all this? Consider how he seeks knowledge of everything except knowledge of God. For instance, his utmost desire is to penetrate the mysteries of the lowest strata of the earth. Day by day he strives to know what can be found ten metres below the surface, what he can discover within the stone, what he can learn by archaeological research in the dust. He puts forth arduous labors to fathom terrestrial mysteries but is not at all concerned about knowing the mysteries of the Kingdom, traversing the illimitable fields of the eternal world, becoming informed of the divine realities, discovering the secrets of God, attaining the knowledge of God, witnessing the splendours of the Sun of Truth and realizing the glories of everlasting life. He is unmindful and thoughtless of these. How much he is attracted to the mysteries of matter, and how completely unaware he is of the mysteries of Divinity! [60]

O thou who art attracted to the Kingdom of God! Every soul seeketh an object and cherisheth a desire, and day and night striveth to attain his aim. One craveth riches, another thirsteth for glory and still another yearneth for fame, for art, for prosperity and the like. Yet finally all are doomed to loss and disappointment. One and all they leave behind them all that is theirs and empty-handed hasten to the realm beyond, and all their labours shall be in vain. To dust they shall all return, denuded, depressed, disheartened and in utter despair.

But, praised be the Lord, thou art engaged in that which secureth for thee a gain that shall eternally endure; and that is naught but thine attraction to the Kingdom of God, thy faith, and thy knowledge, the enlightenment of thine heart, and thine earnest endeavour to promote the Divine Teachings.

Verily this gift is imperishable and this wealth is a treasure from on high![61]

The children of men are all brothers, and the prerequisites of brotherhood are manifold. Among them is that one should wish for one's brother that which one wisheth for oneself. Therefore, it behoveth him who is the recipient of an inward or outward gift or who partaketh of the bread of heaven to inform and invite his friends with the utmost love and kindness. If they respond favourably, his object is attained; otherwise he should leave them to themselves without contending with them or uttering a word that would cause the least sadness.[62]

We are like a piece of iron in the midst of the fire which becomes heated to such a degree that it partakes of the nature of the fire and gives out the same effect to all it touches – so is the soul that is always turned towards God, and filled with the spirit.[63]

That which God – glorified be His Name! – hath desired for Himself is the hearts of His servants, which are the treasuries of His love and remembrance and the repositories of His knowledge and wisdom. It hath ever been the wish of the Eternal King to cleanse the hearts of His servants from the things of the world and all that pertaineth thereunto, that they may be made worthy recipients of the effulgent splendours of Him Who is the King of all names and attributes. Wherefore must no stranger be allowed in the city of the heart, that the incomparable Friend may enter His abode. By this is meant the effulgence of His names and attributes, and not His exalted Essence, inasmuch as that peerless King hath ever been, and shall eternally remain, sanctified above ascent and descent.[64]

Say: If ye be seekers after this life and the vanities thereof, ye should have sought them while ye were still enclosed in your mothers' wombs, for at that time ye were continually approaching them, could ye but perceive it. Ye have, on the other hand, ever since ye were born and attained maturity, been all the while receding from the world and drawing closer to dust. Why, then, exhibit such greed in amassing the treasures of the earth, when your days are numbered and your chance is well-nigh lost? Will ye not, then, O heedless ones, shake off your slumber? [65]

Then know, O thou virtuous soul, that as soon as thou becomest separated from aught else save God and dost cut thyself from the worldly things, thy heart will shine with lights of divinity and with the effulgence of the Sun of Truth from the horizon of the Realm of Might, and then thou wilt be filled by the spirit of power from God and become capable of doing that which thou desirest. This is the confirmed truth.[66]

They say: 'Where is Paradise, and where is Hell?' Say: 'The one is reunion with Me; the other thine own self . . . '[67]

The greatest attainment in the world of humanity is nearness to God.[68]

The purpose of the one true God in manifesting Himself is to summon all mankind to truthfulness and sincerity, to piety and trustworthiness, to resignation and submissiveness to the

Will of God, to forbearance and kindliness, to uprightness and wisdom. His object is to array every man with the mantle of a saintly character, and to adorn him with the ornament of holy and goodly deeds.[69]

. . . strive that your actions day by day may be beautiful prayers. Turn towards God, and seek always to do that which is right and noble. Enrich the poor, raise the fallen, comfort the sorrowful, bring healing to the sick, reassure the fearful, rescue the oppressed, bring hope to the hopeless, shelter the destitute! . . . God, who sees all hearts, knows how far our lives are the fulfillment of our words.[70]

Exultest thou over the treasures thou dost possess, knowing they shall perish? Rejoicest thou in that thou rulest a span of earth, when the whole world, in the estimation of the people of Bahá, is worth as much as the black in the eye of a dead ant? Abandon it unto such as have set their affections upon it, and turn thou unto Him Who is the Desire of the world. Whither are gone the proud and their palaces? Gaze thou into their tombs, that thou mayest profit by this example, in as much as We made it a lesson unto every beholder. Were the breezes of Revelation to seize thee, thou wouldst flee the world, and turn unto the Kingdom, and wouldst expend all thou possessest, that thou mayest draw nigh unto this sublime Vision.[71]

The generations that have gone on before you – whither are they fled? And those round whom in life circled the fairest and the loveliest of the land, where now are they? Profit by their example, O people, and be not of them that are gone astray.

Others ere long will lay hands on what ye possess, and enter into your habitations. Incline your ears to My words, and be not numbered among the foolish.

For every one of you his paramount duty is to choose for himself that on which no other may infringe and none usurp from him. Such a thing – and to this the Almighty is My witness – is the love of God, could ye but perceive it.

Build for yourselves such houses as the rain and floods can never destroy, which shall protect you from the changes and chances of this life. This is the instruction of Him Whom the world hath wronged and forsaken.[72]

Know then that the Lord God possesseth invisible realms which the human intellect can never hope to fathom nor the mind of man conceive. When once thou hast cleansed the channel of thy spiritual sense from the pollution of this worldly life, then wilt thou breathe in the sweet scents of holiness that blow from the blissful bowers of that heavenly land.[73]

The Tongue of Wisdom proclaimeth: He that hath Me not is bereft of all things. Turn ye away from all that is on earth and seek none else but Me. I am the Sun of Wisdom and the Ocean of Knowledge. I cheer the faint and revive the dead. I am the guiding Light that illumineth the way. I am the royal Falcon on the arm of the Almighty. I unfold the drooping wings of every broken bird and start it on its flight.[74]

. . . whoso seeketh to assist God must, before all else, conquer, with the sword of inner meaning and explanation, the city of his own heart and guard it from the remembrance of all save God, and only then set out to subdue the cities of the hearts of others.[75]

Verily, thy Lord assisteth and watcheth over thee at all times and under all conditions.[76]

Know also that the soul is endowed with two wings: should it soar in the atmosphere of love and contentment, then it will be related to the All-Merciful. And should it fly in the atmosphere of self and desire, then it will pertain to the Evil One; may God shield and protect us and protect you therefrom, O ye who perceive![77]

Nowhere doth your true and abiding glory reside except in your firm adherence unto the precepts of God, your wholehearted observance of His laws, your resolution to see that they do not remain unenforced, and to pursue steadfastly the right course.[78]

Know ye of a certainty that all the treasures of the earth, all the gold, the silver, and the rare and precious gems they contain, are, in the sight of God, of His chosen ones and His loved ones, as worthless as a handful of clay. For erelong all that is on earth shall perish, and the kingdom will remain unto God, the All-Powerful, the Incomparable. That which perisheth can never profit Us, nor can it profit you, were ye but to reflect.[79]

. . . man's supreme honour and real happiness lie in self-respect, in high resolves, and noble purposes, in integrity and moral quality, in immaculacy of mind.[80]

Words of Wisdom

In the Name of God, the Exalted, the Most High.

The source of all good is trust in God, submission unto His command, and contentment with His holy will and pleasure.

The essence of wisdom is the fear of God, the dread of His scourge and punishment, and the apprehension of His justice and decree.

The essence of religion is to testify unto that which the Lord hath revealed, and follow that which He hath ordained in His mighty Book.

The source of all glory is acceptance of whatsoever the Lord hath bestowed, and contentment with that which God hath ordained.

The essence of love is for man to turn his heart to the Beloved One, and sever himself from all else but Him, and desire naught save that which is the desire of his Lord.

True remembrance is to make mention of the Lord, the All-Praised, and forget aught else beside Him.

True reliance is for the servant to pursue his profession and calling in this world, to hold fast unto the Lord, to seek naught but His grace, inasmuch as in His Hands is the destiny of all His servants.

The essence of detachment is for man to turn his face towards the courts of the Lord, to enter His Presence, behold His Countenance, and stand as witness before Him.

The essence of understanding is to testify to one's poverty, and submit to the Will of the Lord, the Sovereign, the Gracious, the All-Powerful.

The source of courage and power is the promotion of the Word of God, and steadfastness in His Love.

The essence of charity is for the servant to recount the blessings of his Lord, and to render thanks unto Him at all times and under all conditions.

The essence of faith is fewness of words and abundance of deeds; he whose words exceed his deeds, know verily his death is better than his life.

The essence of true safety is to observe silence, to look at the end of things and to renounce the world.

The beginning of magnanimity is when man expendeth his wealth on himself, on his family and on the poor among his brethren in his Faith.

The essence of wealth is love for Me; whoso loveth Me is the possessor of all things, and he that loveth Me not is indeed of the poor and needy. This is that which the Finger of Glory and Splendour hath revealed.

The source of all evil is for man to turn away from his Lord and set his heart on things ungodly.

The most burning fire is to question the signs of God, to dispute idly that which He hath revealed, to deny Him and carry one's self proudly before Him.

The source of all learning is the knowledge of God, exalted be His Glory, and this cannot be attained save through the knowledge of His Divine Manifestation.

The essence of abasement is to pass out from under the

shadow of the Merciful and seek the shelter of the Evil One.

The source of error is to disbelieve in the One true God, rely upon aught else but Him, and flee from His Decree.

True loss is for him whose days have been spent in utter ignorance of his self.

The essence of all that We have revealed for thee is Justice, is for man to free himself from idle fancy and imitation, discern with the eye of oneness His glorious handiwork, and look into all things with a searching eye.

Thus have We instructed thee, manifested unto thee Words of Wisdom, that thou mayest be thankful unto the Lord, thy God, and glory therein amidst all peoples.[81]

16

HEALING MEDITATION

Our true nature is peaceful and joyous. However, as we go through the journey of life, most of us lose the joy and peace with which we were born. A major part of this change from the 'original condition' is the negative habits of the mind that are developed during our life's journey. Such habits can colour and influence our perspective of life, thus leading to both physical and mental illnesses. While medication can heal many physical illnesses, we can also experiment with non-chemical treatments for other types of illnesses, especially those affecting one's mind or spirit:

> There are two ways of healing diseases, the material and the spiritual way. The first is the remedies of the physicians; the second prayers and turning one's self to God. Both must be practised and followed. The diseases that happen to be caused by physical accident are cured by medical aid; others, which are due to spiritual causes, will disappear by spiritual means. For instance: For a disease due to grieving, fear, nervous impressions, the spiritual remedies will take more effect than the physical. Therefore, these two kinds of remedies must be followed; neither is an obstacle to the other . . . And if thou art looking for the divine remedy which will cure the spirit of man of all diseases and make him obtain the health of the divine Kingdom, know that it is the precepts and teachings of God. Take the greatest care of them. [1]

Threats to our safety can create fear, anxiety and stress. There is a part of our central nervous system known as the sympathetic nervous system (SNS) that is responsible for automated responses to such threats. When we face physical threats, our SNS will instantly 'rev up' the body in preparation to help us either flee from the danger zone or stay and fight with the threat. It does so by increasing the supply of blood and oxygen to the body: we begin to breathe heavier. Our heart beats faster to pump more blood into our bloodstreams. Our muscles tense up in preparation for quick moves. Our bladder and bowel activity is increased to free the body for strenuous activity. A higher dose of adrenaline is also pumped into our bloodstream to give us additional stamina and strength to execute the 'fight or flight' response. Even our pupils dilate to enhance our vision for facing the danger. When the threat is removed, another part of our central nervous system known as the parasympathetic nervous system (PSNS) will calm the body down to its pre-threat conditions.

Interestingly, the Bahá'í Writings appear to indicate that the powers of the SNS that responds to threats are not entirely physical:

> The powers of the sympathetic nerve are neither entirely physical nor spiritual, but are between the two (systems). The nerve is connected with both. Its phenomena shall be perfect when its spiritual and physical relations are normal.
>
> When the material world and the divine world are well co-related, when the hearts become heavenly and the aspirations grow pure and divine, perfect connection shall take place. Then shall this power produce a perfect manifestation. Physical and spiritual diseases will then receive absolute healing.[2]

According to 'Abdu'l-Bahá, we can train ourselves through spiritual means to control our responses to fear, anxiety and depression. While it is always a safe practice to flee from an attacking lion, we don't have to 'flee' from all stressful conditions. We can learn to effectively fight depression and fears and gradually regain our natural balance by engaging in the practice of healing meditations, which can provide us with a deep state of both physical and psychological relaxation. Healing meditations neutralize the impact of stress. They can also create conditions in which our body's immune system and its innate healing powers function at their best.[3]

There are four healing powers or qualities of mind that we can bring to this type of meditation: positive images, positive words, positive feelings and positive belief. Having 'positive belief' is the real foundation. Here, belief is not blind faith. Rather, it is an understanding, knowledge and assurance that our mind can release its own healing power by means of images, words and feelings. The true source of healing lies in our own minds.[4]

When we seek healing, it is important to reach out to a divine Source or Presence that inspires warmth, peace and joy. This Being can be visualized in our mind's eye as pure light. The use of light in healing meditations can indeed assist us in drawing upon untapped strength that we already have. In religious traditions such as Buddhism, light is viewed as the most potent means for healing and obtaining blessings. [5]

One way to practise light imagery for healing the body and mind is to imagine the light showering down on us, filling us entirely with its warmth and healing. In our mind's eye, we can even feel that the heat of the light is melting our problem areas, thus bringing us peace and joy. We can also imagine every part of our body being effortlessly filled with this glorious light. By the end of the practice, we can see ourselves transformed into a body of light free from physical or mental problems. [6]

Significance of Light in the World's Religions

His beauty hath no veiling save light, His face no covering save revelation.[7]

The idea of a radiant, glorious and effulgent light as the closest phenomenon on earth to the divine seems to be present in one form or another in all the major religions of the world. This light is not only the source of creation and authority in the world of existence, it is also the source of spiritual guidance to the true believer.[8] In many religions, in addition to God, the prophets, holy scripture, and religion itself have also been likened to the Light:

> The sacred literature of different religions is replete with men-tions of the concept of light as the vanquisher of darkness and the source of guidance for humanity. At different times, God, prophets, the religion itself or its holy Book have all been likened unto a light that shines in the darkness of our earthly existence to illuminate the treacherous road to salvation and liberation. At times, the focus is on the very source of light – God Himself. More frequently, though, it is the prophet who is presented as the beacon of light to humankind. This is probably due to the fact that we can better identify with prophets who appear in our likeness as fellow humans and can be physically experienced than with a transcendent being like God whom we have no conception of.
>
> Close examination of the lives of the divine educators reveals that, through their words and deeds, these holy person-alities have indeed served as sources of guidance to others. In the process, they have sacrificed their comfort, their material possessions, and at times their very lives to enlighten and save others. By accepting countless sufferings, even tragic deaths, they provide powerful examples of the ideal human being, inspiring their contemporaries and later generations.[9]

Early Zoroastrian creation myths depict Satan (Ahriman) as sitting in darkness unaware of the existence of God (Ahura Mazda). Then Satan beholds God's first indications in the distance as a gradu-ally increasing light. He then learns that this Being of Light is Ahura Mazda, who is the source of all good and the Creator of the universe. In the Zoroastrian tradition, this light is also the divine essence of the prophet-founder, Zarathustra (Zoroaster).[10]

In Hinduism, the Vedic literature views God (Brahman) as Light. The same idea finds support in the Bhagavad Gita:

He is the light of all lights which shines beyond all darkness. It is vision, the end of vision, to be reached by vision, dwelling in the heart of all.[11]

He who remembers the Poet, the Creator, who rules all things from all time, smaller than the smallest atom, but upholding this vast universe, who shines like the sun beyond darkness, far far beyond human thoughts; and at the time of his departure is in union of love and the power of Yoga and, with a mind that wanders not, keeps the power of his life between his eyebrows, he goes to that Spirit Supreme, the Supreme Spirit of Light.[12]

Supreme Brahman, Light supreme, and supreme purification, Spirit divine eternal, unborn God from the beginning, omnipresent Lord of all.[13]

If the light of a thousand suns suddenly arose in the sky, that splendour might be compared to the radiance of the Supreme Spirit.[14]

And even as one sun gives light to all things in this world, so the Lord of the field gives light to all his field.[15]

Other passages in the Bhagavad Gita present Krishna as a source of light to the world.

By my grace and my wondrous power I have shown to thee Arjuna[16] this form supreme made of light, which is the Infinite, the All: mine own form from the beginning, never seen by man before.[17]

That splendour of light that comes from the sun and which illumines the whole universe, the soft light of the moon, the brightness of fire – know that they all come from me.[18]

In Buddhism, Buddha is presented as a guiding light that shines in the darkness of this world of existence.

> So long as a Tathagata arises not, an Arahat, a Buddha Supreme, there is no shining forth of great light, of great radiance, but gross darkness of bewilderment prevails, and there is no proclamation of the Four Noble Truths, no teaching, no showing forth, no setting up, no opening up, no analysis, no making plain.
>
> But, brethren, as soon as a Tathagata arises in the world, then there is a shining forth of great light, of great radiance. Then is there no more gloom and darkness of bewilderment; then is there a proclamation of the Four Noble Truths; then is there teaching, a shining forth, a setting up, an opening up, an analysis, a making plain.[19]

In Judaism too, God is likened to a light:

> The Lord is my light and my salvation; whom shall I fear? The Lord is the strength of my life; of whom shall I be afraid?[20]

In another place, the author of Psalms compares the Word of God to a lamp and light that guides his steps:

> Thy word is a lamp to my feet, and a light to my path.[21]

In Proverbs, God's commandments are compared to a lamp and His teachings to a light:

> For the commandment is a lamp and the teaching a light; and reproofs of instruction are the way of life.[22]

Isaiah considers the Lord as the everlasting light of Zion (the seat of the Lord's reign, figurative Jerusalem or Israel):

> The sun shall be no more your light by day; nor for brightness

shall the moon give light to you by night, but the Lord will be your everlasting glory. Your sun shall no more go down, nor your moon withdraw itself; for the Lord will be your everlasting light, and your days of mourning shall be ended.[23]

In the Jewish mystical tradition known as Kabbalah, God is called *Ein Sof,* which means the 'Infinite Light':

One of the celebrated Kabbalists of sixteenth-century Safed, Rabbi Eliezer Ezcary, writes of a technique that involves meditating on the divine energy of the shechinah[24] hovering overhead and imagining this all-encompassing, loving light pervading the immediate space until the meditator envisions himself dwelling in the heart of this light.[25]

In the Christian Bible, the Father (God) has in some instances been identified with light:

Every good gift and every perfect gift is from above, and cometh down from the Father of lights, with whom is no variableness, neither shadow of turning.[26]

This then is the message which we have heard of him, and declare unto you, that God is light, and in him is no darkness at all.[27]

However, it is the Son (Jesus) who is more frequently presented as the Light of the world:

There was a man sent from God, whose name was John. He came for testimony, to bear witness to the light, that all might believe through him. He was not the light, but came to bear witness to the light. The true light that enlightens every man was coming into the world. He was in the world, and the world was made through him, yet the world knew him not.[28]

And this is the judgement, that the light [Jesus] has come into the world, and men loved darkness rather than light, because their deeds were evil.[29]

For God, who commanded the light to shine out of darkness, hath shined in our hearts, to give the light of the knowledge of the glory of God in the face of Jesus Christ.[30]

And the city had no need of the sun, neither of the moon, to shine in it: for the glory of God did lighten it, and the Lamb [Jesus] is the light thereof.[31]

In the following passages, Christ considers Himself to be the light of this world:

As long as I am in the world, I am the light of the world.[32]

I have come as light into the world, that whoever believes in me may not remain in darkness.[33]

I am the light of the world; he who follows me will not walk in darkness, but will have the light of life.[34]

Jesus said to them, 'The light is with you for a little longer. Walk while you have the light, lest the darkness overtake you; he who walks in the darkness does not know where he goes. While you have the light, believe in the light, that you may become sons of light.'[35]

In the Qur'án, an entire chapter is devoted to the concept of light. In the chapter, God is considered to be the light of the universe:

God is the light of the heavens and of the earth. His light is like a niche in which is a lamp-the lamp encased in glass – the glass, as it were, a glistening star. From a blessed tree is it lighted, the olive neither of the East nor of the West, whose oil would well nigh shine out, even though fire touched it not! It is light upon light. God guideth whom He will to His light, and God setteth forth parables to men, for God knoweth all things.[36]

Some Quranic passages seem to point to the Islamic revelation as the light:

O men! Now hath a proof come to you from your Lord and we have sent down to you a clear light.[37]

Fain would they put out the light of God with their mouths! But though the infidels hate it, God will perfect His light.[38]

And those who shall believe in him [Muhammad] and strengthen him and help him, and follow the light which hath been sent down with him – these are they with whom it shall be well.[39]

Believe then in God and His Apostle and in the Light which We have sent down; for God is fully aware of all ye do.[40]

Other Quranic verses declare the Qur'án itself as the light of guidance:

And thus, too (O Muhammad) have We revealed unto thee a life-giving message, (coming) at our behest . . . We have caused this (message) to be a light, whereby We guide whom We will of our servants.[41]

O people of the Scriptures! now is Our Apostle come to you to clear up to you much that ye concealed of those Scriptures and to pass over many things. Now hath a light and a clear Book come to you from God, by which God will guide him who shall follow after His good pleasure, to paths of peace, and will bring them out of the darkness to the light, by His will: and to the straight path will He guide them.[42]

In addition to the Qur'án, there is a prayer attributed to the Prophet Muhammad that focuses on light, This prayer was loved by Rumi, the great Muslim mystic, and is a favourite prayer of Mevlevi dervishes.[43]

O God! Grant me Light in my heart, Light in my grave,
Light in front of me, Light behind me,
Light to my right, Light to my left,
Light above me, Light below me, Light in my ears, Light in my eyes,
Light on my skin, Light in my hair,
Light within my flesh, Light in my blood, Light in my bones.
O God! Increase my Light everywhere.
O God! Grant me Light in my heart,
Light on my tongue, Light in my eyes, Light in my ears,
Light to my right, Light to my left,
Light above me, Light below me,
Light in front of me, Light behind me,
and Light within my self; increase my Light.[44]

The concept of light in Muslim tradition was further developed in Iranian Sufism. Shihab ad-Din Suhrawardi (d. 1191), a great philosopher/mystic, speaks of a glorious, radiant, and effulgent light that emits from the sun. He even has a hymn to the sun as 'the vanquisher of darkness' and is first to present metaphysics of light:

> God is the 'light of lights' (*núr al-anwár*), and everything else possesses a differing lesser intensity of light. The status of any entity thus depends on how close they are to the 'light of lights' and how much they are consequently illuminated by it. That which is the closest to the God is pure light while increasing darkness denotes materiality and distance from the Divine. It is important to realise that this metaphysics of light was the result not so much of a system of philosophy that Suhrawardi had arrived at by rational thought, but rather was based upon his mystical visions, which he then rationalised and systematised.[45]

Suhrawardi's soul yearned for spiritual communion with his Beloved:

> Thou, my lord and prince, my most holy angel, my precious spiritual being . . . Thou who art clothed in the most brilliant of divine Lights . . . may Thou manifest Thyself to me in the most beautiful of epiphanies. Show me the light of Thy dazzling face, be for me the mediator . . . lift the veils of darkness from my heart.[46]

In the Bábí Faith, there are many passages that refer to the concept of light. For instance, the Báb identified Himself with both the light that is found in the Quranic chapter 'Light', as well as the light that appeared in the Burning Bush to Moses when He was appointed to prophethood.[47]

> I am the Lamp which the Finger of God hath lit within its niche and caused to shine with deathless splendour. I am the Flame of that supernal Light that glowed upon Sinai in the gladsome Spot, and lay concealed in the midst of the Burning Bush.[48]

In the following quotations the Báb further elucidates the concept of divine light and its relationship to the realm of humanity:

> This is . . . the Light above every light . . . Indeed every light is generated by God through the power of His behest. He of a truth is the Light in the kingdom of heaven and earth and whatever is between them. Through the radiance of His light God imparteth illumination to your hearts and maketh firm your steps, that perchance ye may yield praise unto Him.[49]

> The One True God may be compared unto the sun and the believer unto a mirror. No sooner is the mirror placed before the sun than it reflects its light.[50]

In the Bahá'í Faith, the concept of light is an important theme. Numerous passages identify God as the heavenly light:

Thy glory beareth me witness, O Thou, the Light of the world! The fire of Thy love that burneth continually within me hath so inflamed me that whoever among Thy creatures approacheth me, and inclineth his inner ear towards me, cannot fail to hear its raging within each of my veins.[51]

. . . within every atom are enshrined the signs that bear eloquent testimony to the revelation of that Most Great Light.[52]

Deprive me not, O my Lord, of the splendours of the light of Thy Face, whose brightness hath illuminated the whole world.[53]

I have turned my face unto Thee, O my Lord! Illumine it with the light of Thy countenance. Protect it, then, from turning to anyone but Thee.[54]

'They [Prophets] all proceed from the same Light.'[55]

Withhold not from me, O my Lord, the things thou didst ordain for such of Thy handmaidens . . . on whom are poured continually the splendours of the sun of Thy beauty and the beams of the brightness of Thy face.[56]

The All-loving God created man to radiate the Divine light and to illumine the world by his words, action, and life.[57]
. . . my Refuge, and my Light . . . O Thou Light of Light! O Thou Light above all Lights![58]

Praise be to God Who hath caused the Light to circle round the twin Mounts of His Light and made the Light to revolve around the twin Spheres of His Light. He hath caused the Light to beam forth in the Loci of His Light and made the

Light to be retained in the Repositories of His Light.

He hath also caused the Light to scintillate through the impulses of His Light and made the Light to shine resplendent in the Countenances of His Light. Praise God! Praised be God! Worthy of praise is He Who establisheth His Own worth, for besides Him there is none other. [59]

Other passages in the Bahá'í Holy Texts present Bahá'u'lláh's revelation as the divine Light that guides the human race:

But God, having stayed their hands, revealed this Light through His sovereign authority and protected it through the power of His might until earth and heaven were illumined by its radiance and brightness.[60]

Say: 'The light hath shone forth from the horizon of Revelation, and the whole earth hath been illumined at the coming of Him Who is the Lord of the Day of the Covenant!'[61]

O Bethlehem! This Light hath risen in the orient, and traveled towards the occident, until it reached thee in the evening of its life.[62]

Say: In the East the Light of His Revelation hath broken; in the West the signs of His dominion have appeared.[63]

Then, there are passages that point to Bahá'u'lláh Himself as the Light of guidance:

Behold, then, O my God, how Thy Light hath been compassed with the onrushing winds of Thy decree.[64]

. . . in Persian Iraq, he first heard the uproar caused by the Advent of the Most Great Light . . . [65]

We, in truth, have sent Him Whom We aided with the Holy

Spirit [Jesus Christ] that He may announce unto you this Light that hath shone forth from the horizon of the Will of your Lord, the Most Exalted, the All-Glorious, and Whose signs have been revealed in the West.[66]

Verily, this is the Point which God hath ordained to be an ocean of light for the sincere among His servants and a flame of fire to the froward amidst His creatures and the impious among His people . . . [67]

Indeed He is a Light which is not followed by darkness and a Truth not overtaken by error.[68]

O Emperor of Austria! He Who is the Dayspring of God's Light dwelt in the prison of 'Akká at the time when thou didst set forth to visit the Aqsá Mosque [Jerusalem].[69]

Significance of Light in the Near-Death Experience

The radiance of the brightest luminaries is eclipsed by the effulgent splendours of Thy face . . . [70]

The concept of light also plays a significant role in the near-death experience (NDE) phenomenon, where many of those who have undergone this speak of people of light, a realm of light and a Being of Light in whose presence they find extraordinary joy and peace. According to Dr Raymond Moody, who is probably the best-known figure in the field of NDE, people who have a near-death experience usually fall into one of two broad categories: those 'who were resuscitated after having been . . . pronounced clinically dead by their doctors'; and people 'who, in the course of accidents or severe injury or illness, came very close to physical death'.[71]

People of Light

The people of light are beings who glow with great luminescence. They come to meet and greet the person at the end of a tunnel during their near-death experience and fill them with love. The light that emanates from the people of light has been described by some of those who have experienced it as the purest form of love. In spite of its intensity, this light is not painful to the viewer's eye. On the contrary, it is very warm, pleasant and vibrant. The people of light are often deceased family members, relatives or friends of the person undergoing NDE, who communicate with them telepathically.[72]

> Today, under the shadowing mercy of God, he [Sháh-Muhammad-Amin] dwells in the bright Heavens. He communes with the birds of holiness, and in the assemblage of splendours he is immersed in light.[73]

> [Muhammad Haná-Sáb] died, and hastened onward to the world of lights, to the assemblage where the beauty of God is unveiled.[74]

Being of Light

Most people with an NDE experience also report an encounter with a kind and loving Being of Light who welcomes them into the world beyond. This Being seems to know everything about them and has immense understanding and compassion for them. Their encounter is so amazing that they cannot easily describe it in words:

> It did seem that it was a little dim at first, but then it was this huge beam. It was just a tremendous amount of light, nothing like a big bright flash light, it was just too much light. And it gave off heat to me; I felt a warm sensation. It was a bright yellowish white —more white. It was tremendously bright;

I just can't describe it. It seemed to cover everything, yet it didn't prevent me from seeing everything around me . . . From the moment the light spoke to me, I felt really good-secure and loved. The love which came from it is just unimaginable, indescribable.[75]

The Being of Light radiates total love and appears to religious and non-religious people alike. For the religious, their faith and orientation appears to impact how they see the Being of Light. Thus, Christians may see the Light as Jesus, Buddhists as Buddha, and Bahá'ís as Bahá'u'lláh. Others simply identify the Being as God,[76] while painters have also attempted to portray the experience (see photograph section).

17

VISUALIZATION

Where there is no vision, the people perish.

Proverbs[1]

In addition to meditation and prayer, visualization too can affect the brain. A study conducted at Yale University found that visualization can stimulate almost all the same areas of our brain as meditation techniques do.[2]

Using visualization can be of paramount importance in healing the body. Numerous studies show that the human nervous system is influenced by our mental state. The images we create and see in our mind's eye during visualization are capable of affecting the physiology of our bodies, thus leading us back to health and healing. In the course of visualization, the more profoundly we experience the imagery, the more our body's physiology will change:

> Edmund Jacobsen, the renowned physiologist, demonstrated extensively that when people imagine body movements, the motor nerves in these areas actually fire and the muscle fibers contract. These movements, called micromovements, can be very subtle, but even if they are not visible to the eye, they can be picked up by electromyographic machines. This response is remarkable in itself, but even more interesting is the fact that the body builds nerve circuits, that is, it 'learns', based on imagery exercises that result in micromovements. This learning is the basis of the imagery exercises that athletes use to improve their performance. When they picture successful completion

of an activity, their performance actually improves. The micro-movements improve the athletes' performance as they increase the athletes' confidence in their ability to perform. Imagery has also been shown to have immediate physiological effects on body systems other than the muscles. It directly affects the gastrointestinal tract . . . imagery affects virtually every organ in the body.[3]

In addition to healing, you can use visualization for connecting to your inner core and cultivating such qualities as love, forgiveness, patience, inner peace, compassion and wisdom. Alternatively, you can simply use this technique for stress reduction and inner relaxation. To use visualization for stress release, create images in your mind that will make you feel calm and peaceful. For instance, visualize a secret place in the mind; a place where you can be happy and at ease. It could be a place you have been to before or just something you create in your mind. Spend some time working on all the details of the place. You can also create a sacred space such as a temple or a sanctuary within your heart where you can go during prayer and meditation, or any time you need to have some inner peace and serenity.[4]

You can carry out visualizations during breaks at work, at home, as you go out into nature, when you are in a bus or on a plane. But don't do them while driving or operating machinery. Sit in a chair or just lie down with a light blanket to keep yourself warm, as your body temperature drops during visualization. Listening to soothing music can enhance your experience. Before you start, loosen your belt if you're wearing one, and take off your watch and glasses (if you can). Your visualization can be as short as five minutes or as long as 20 to 30 minutes.[5]

Examples of Visualization for Relaxation

Inner Sanctuary

We must make our heart a spiritual temple wherein to adore Him incessantly.[6]

One day, I was contemplating on the meaning of the above passage and the expression 'spiritual temple' caught my attention. I began visualizing this spiritual temple inside of me as an 'inner sanctuary' I could journey to throughout the day to be with my Beloved. Gradually, I developed a visualization meditation routine which has been particularly helpful to me:

Imagine you are sitting in a beautiful place in nature, surrounded by flowering trees in the shape of a circle around you. You are sitting on a soft, fluffy surface in the middle of the circle next to a fountain. You feel like you're almost sitting on a cloud. The trees around you are in full bloom, with a wide array of pink peach blossom, yellow flowering Senna, white pear blossom and orange pomegranate blossom. You are accompanied by singing birds including red robins, yellow canaries, and white and blue birds sitting in the trees. A gentle, cool breeze is blowing over your face, which makes you feel even more relaxed. A magnificent Light is also shining on your face from above, but the Light is gentle and soothing. You feel safe and secure in this Light when you turn to it and, with love and adoration, say His Name (your mantra) as you smile, remembering this biblical verse: 'in Thy presence there is fullness of joy'.[7]

You can recall this simple visualization to 'escape' from mundane or annoying things in life like getting stuck in traffic, waiting at the doctor's office, or experiencing delays at the airport. I can still vividly recall the first time I experimented with the Inner Sanctuary visualization outside my meditation room. I had gone to the dentist, where I was told the procedure might end up being more complicated than they had originally anticipated, and they said I had to sign some paperwork before they would carry out the procedure. At first, I felt a little apprehensive. Then, I said to myself that I can *go to my Inner Sanctuary* and engage in repeating my mantra, the Greatest Name, during the entire procedure.

For the next hour, I was visualizing myself in my Inner Sanctuary, surrounded by the blossoming trees with singing birds, and in communion with the Beloved as the Light. I would lovingly reach out to Him through His Name and implore His Grace. At other times, I saw myself sitting by what I describe as the *Pond of Serenity*, a pond with crystal clear, still water in scenic nature and, turning to Him, recited His Name. For me, the image of a serene pond reinforced stillness of mind (see photograph section). Alternating between the Inner Sanctuary and the Pond of Serenity brought so much peace to my mind and joy to my heart that I didn't feel the passage of time or worry about the procedure as the dentist worked on my teeth. I left his office feeling really peaceful. I attribute a lot of that to the power of His Name and the soothing impact of the visualization techniques I used.

A walk in the countryside

Visualize yourself walking down a country lane in the summer afternoon sun, listening to the birds singing, smelling the sweet air – bring all your senses into the visualization. Then you come to a gate, and when you go through it you enter the most beautiful garden with luxuriant flowers, shady trees and a soft lawn. Bees are humming, birds darting at the edge of a wild pond, a few swans swim past and the air is laden with summer scents. You are completely at ease here; you are safe, relaxed and feel great happiness.[8]

The house of tranquillity

You are walking on a path. You are relaxed, peaceful, and content. You are dressed comfortably and the temperature is just right, not too cold or too warm. You are enjoying being in nature. You can feel the warmth of the sun and a gentle breeze.

You can hear the sweet chirping of birds. The fresh air tastes and smells clean and refreshing. As you walk along the path you begin to see a house on the path. You decide to go to this house, and you understand somehow that this house has been waiting just for you. As you approach, notice the details of the outside of the house . . . Walk now to the front door. The door swings open just as you are ready to turn the knob. You are filled with the certainty that this house is for you, just for you. Step inside now and notice all the details of the interior . . . Now that you are well acquainted with your house, decide what you might like to do next . . . listen to music . . . make a cup of tea . . . Gently now, you realize that it is time to return to your path . . . Understand that this house . . . will always be waiting for you anytime you wish, and it will always contain . . . what you need.[9]

Waterfall and light visualization

Take three deep breaths. Sit comfortably with your eyes closed. And as you are smiling, imagine that you are sitting under the shade of a beautiful tree in a peaceful lagoon with a gentle waterfall (see photograph section). Hear the cascade of water as it showers over rocks. Approach the waterfall and stand beneath it. Feel the inner peace as the refreshing water is washing over you. If there are pain areas in your body, as you are standing beneath the waterfall, recite the Greatest Name mentally. Feel the warm water pouring over your body. You can imagine the pain areas being covered with mud. As you invoke His Name, feel the water washing away the mud off the pain area until you become hollow. Then in your mind's eye see yourself standing in the presence of a magnificent Light. Continue with your invocation of the Greatest Name and as you are mentally reciting it, feel the rays of the Light filling your hollow body from head to toe until you become a body of light. Smile.

Creative Visualization

> For truly, I say to you, if you have faith as a grain of mustard seed, you will say to this mountain, 'Move hence to yonder place', and it will move; and nothing will be impossible to you.[10]

Another form of visualization is creative visualization, which can be of great benefit for the attainment of our objectives in life. In her book *Creative Visualization*, Shakti Gawain suggests four main steps:

1. Set a goal.
2. Provide your mind with a vivid picture of your objective with as many details as you would like to.
3. Regularly concentrate on the mental picture you have created.
4. Strengthen the image by making encouraging and positive statements to yourself. [11]

Clearly express your desired visualization goal in speech and in writing. Write the goal on a piece of paper and post it in a place where you can view it daily. It is scientifically proven that the longer you focus on this image in your mind, the more real it begins to feel to you. For instance, if you spend a long time focusing on peace, then your body will begin to feel peaceful and relaxed.[12]

You can make creative visualization a routine part of your daily life. For instance, practise it once or twice a day, preferably when waking up in the morning and before going to sleep at night. These are the times when such visualization can be most effective.[13]

Start with thirty minutes, but as you gain more experience, you can reduce the amount to just a few minutes. It is not the length of time you spend on visualization that makes the difference, but the enthusiasm, faith and belief in the success of the practice.[14] Your visualization sessions should be something you look forward to rather than an unpleasant duty. During the visualization session you need to be relaxed. As you relax, your brain waves change and become more prepared to accept the suggestions you give them.[15]

There are no short cuts to developing habits; they always take time. This is particularly true if the habit is mind-related. Therefore, patience and perseverance are the key elements for making creative visualization a success.

If you think you are not progressing fast enough, give your mind a break for a few days. When you feel you are ready, return to the practice. Keep the creative visualization to yourself. Negative remarks by others are always a possibility, and could hinder your progress.[16]

To use creative visualization for healing certain physical pains, create the ideal image (restored health) in your mind. Next, make some positive statements either out loud or silently to yourself about the visualization. If during the session you are faced with contradictory thoughts, do not fight them. Let them pass by like clouds in the sky. Resisting such thoughts will only give them life. Simply bring your mind back to the ideal image and the positive statements you have formed. A key factor in creative visualization is having a relaxed attitude and enjoying the whole experience.

18

DAILY MEDITATION AND VISUALIZATION

This chapter provides suggestions for daily exercises in meditation and visualization. Although a majority of them are inspired by Bahá'í scriptural passages, it should be emphasized that they are simply suggestions – they are not prescribed practices in the Bahá'í teachings.

The Land of the Beloved

The following mantra meditation is focused on God's Name and His Presence. It has three elements:

 * recitation of the Greatest Name;
 * visualization; and
 * supplication.

This mantra meditation should be practised for 20 minutes once or twice a day. It can lead to spiritual felicity and a sense of peacefulness. During the meditation, if you notice that your mind is wandering, gently and lovingly bring it back to the task at hand. You can think of your mind as a child you take out for a walk. Children are often fascinated by things happening around them and are thus easily distracted. So, imagine your mind as that child. He sees a butterfly and shakes your hand loose to go catch the butterfly. Next, he sees a beautiful flower. Again, he tries to let go of your grasp so he can get closer to the flower and smell or pick it. The same happens to the 'child' of your mind. When you try to concentrate on a meditative task, your mind keeps resisting the discipline, especially if you are new to meditation. This is completely natural. Over time, you will learn to control the mind's wanderings. But you must be patient and steadfast during the early phases.

You should therefore be ready for the frequent wanderings of your mind, and each time gently call the mind back in a sweet and loving manner as you would with the child. Never get upset or frustrated. You can also imagine the distractions as clouds. As unwanted thoughts arise in your mind, let them pass by as clouds in the sky and patiently bring your attention back to meditation. Do your very best to smile through the entire session.

Now let us begin:

Since the focus of our meditation is God's Presence and His Blessed Name, repeat the following verse at least three times with your palms turned up on your lap. Pay close attention to the Sacred Words as you utter them. Ensure that they are *really* coming from the depth of your heart:

> O Lord my God . . . let Thy remembrance be my companion, and Thy love my aim, . . . and Thy name my lamp, and Thy wish my desire.[1]

You can use prayer beads to help you concentrate on the mantra (the Greatest Name). Continue with the mantra meditation by outwardly repeating 'Ya-Bahá'u'l-Abhá' for a few minutes, then lower your voice and begin whispering the mantra and finally end with mental recitation of the Greatest Name. Giving your mind variety will prevent it from boredom. Saying your mantra aloud will help to block out potential sounds and distractions around you. Saying it in your mind is important because it takes focused concentration, which is what you need to discipline the mind. Once you learn to say the mantra internally, you can recall it anytime and anywhere. This will particularly come in handy in times of test and trouble, when you can engage in the practice to draw strength from it without anyone around you noticing.

Here are some suggested visualizations that can be helpful during this stage of your meditation:

As you are repeating the Greatest Name out loud, try to feel the presence of the Holy Spirit in your meditation place. Think of God's Words: 'whenever thou shalt long for Me, thou shalt find Me close to thee,'[2] or 'nigh is he unto such as commune with Him.'[3]

Continue repeating your mantra aloud and as you are doing so, feel that all the atoms of your being are engaged in glorification and praise of the Lord. You can think of these verses of Bahá'u'lláh: 'O my Well-Beloved! Every limb of my body, methinks, is endowed with a tongue that glorifieth Thee and magnifieth Thy name,'[4] or 'every single member of their bodies intoned Thy praise and vibrated to Thy remembrance'.[5]

Now begin whispering 'Ya-Bahá'u'l-Abhá' for a couple of minutes. This time, hear the mantra as you are repeating it. Pay close attention to the sound of your voice. Next, move to the mental recitation of the Greatest Name. You can come up with your own method for this mental recitation, or use one of these two techniques:

- See the letters of the Greatest Name being continuously written with gold ink on a large piece of black velvet in the most exquisite calligraphy.
- Hear the Greatest Name recited in your mind gently and repeatedly.

Spend ten minutes on the mantra meditation. After completing this part, you are now ready to move onto the second part of your session: visualization. You can base this part on a well-known excerpt from a Hidden Word of Bahá'u'lláh: 'Whither can a lover go but to the land of his beloved?'[6]

In your mind's eye, see that you are entering a beautiful place in nature. This place serves as a mental model for the abstract notion of the 'land of the beloved' where nothing is seen or heard but praise and glorification of God. As you enter, you first see the Pond of Serenity (see photograph section, and description in Chapter 17) where you sit to quiet your mind like the water in the pond. This practice reminds you of the Psalm 'Be still and know that I am God.'[7] Feel free to go back and forth between the visualization of the Pond of Serenity and the mental recitation of the Greatest Name.

Next, you leave the pond and arrive at a river where you can hear the Greatest Name in the flow of the water. There, you are surrounded by trees that reach out to the Greatest Name through the warmth of the sun and hear colourful birds singing praises of the Greatest Name. Then, you begin looking around the landscape and see various elements such as rivers, flowers, and trees all engaged in the invocation of God.[8] As you continue walking in the beautiful surroundings, you notice a dazzling, magnificent Light. Walk towards the Light, turn your face to the Light and feel it illuminating your face. Allow the warmth of God's love to enter your being, and smile.

Then, address Him with the following verse from Baha'u'llah: 'Let the object of mine ardent quest be Thy most resplendent, Thine adorable and ever-blessed Beauty.'[9] As you do so, feel His light and warmth covering you. Feel protected and safe in His Light, and smile. Ask Him to enable you through His Grace to know yourself, to uncover the virtues that are latent within your soul and to live a life that is pleasing in His sight.[10]

Continue your supplication by asking Him to protect you against your lower nature and not to leave you to yourself.[11]

Ask Him to help you stay in a continuous state of communion with Him throughout the day[12] as you reach out to Him through prayer, supplication, and the utterance of His Name that 'turneth restlessness into tranquillity, fear into confidence'.[13]

The last part of this meditation involves the imagery of reunion with the Beloved. In your mind's eye, see yourself walking further towards the Light as you are repeating the Greatest Name mentally. Hear Him say, 'Here am I, here am I.' As you enter the Light, feel His loving warmth while you say in your heart, 'I have found . . . no tranquillity except in reunion with Thee.'[14]

Bedtime Visualization

As noted earlier in this book, Bahá'ís are encouraged to begin and end their day with God's name on their lips:

> . . . with whom will he commune at the hour of repose, and whose name will he invoke when riseth from slumber?[15]

So instead of ending your day with a focus on the problems you experienced during the day, or worrying about the challenges lying ahead tomorrow, you might like to try the following.

Visualize yourself sleeping either under a beautiful canopy[16] or in your favourite place of repose. It could be a tropical island, or a bed in nature in the middle of a forest where you are surrounded by trees, flowers, birds and waterfalls. Whatever scenery or setting you choose, try to stay with it for at least a few months. Close your eyes and see yourself in that place of rest. Look around and enjoy the surroundings. Begin to feel the warm presence of the Beloved with you and recite: 'my Refuge, and my Light . . . O Thou Light of Light!'[17] Then continue with the following verse:

> I have committed, O my Lord, my spirit and my entire being into the right hand of Thy might and Thy protection . . . [18]

Continue with a verbal recitation, followed by a mental recitation. Finally, in your mind's eye, see the Greatest Name being written on a piece of black velvet with gold ink, or some other surface over and over again until you fall asleep. Try to fall asleep with the Greatest Name on your lips. Feel assured that: 'Verily, thy Lord assisteth and watcheth over thee at all times and under all conditions.'[19]

Visualization for Overcoming Negative Thoughts and Emotions

As humans, we often struggle with negative thoughts and emotions. We wish they would go away but sometimes they don't, or they don't go away as quickly as we would like. We may want to draw strength from certain scriptural passages when we face temptations or negative thoughts. For example:

> Watch over yourselves, for the Evil One [man's lower or animal nature] is lying in wait, ready to entrap you. Gird yourselves against his wicked devices and, led by the light of the name of the All-Seeing God, make your escape from the darkness that surroundeth you.[20]

> They . . . seek at every moment to journey from the plane of heedlessness into the realm of being.[21]

> Hence, if it should happen that a prompting from Satan stirs thee up (to blind anger), seek refuge with God; behold, He alone is all-hearing, all-knowing.[22]

> Verily, those who fear God, when some phantom from Satan toucheth them, remember Him, and lo! They see clearly.[23]

The Importance of Smiling in your Meditation and Visualization Practice

> Rejoice in the gladness of thine heart, that thou mayest be worthy to meet Me and to mirror forth My beauty.[24]

Another approach to inner joy and peace is regular smiling, even when we don't feel like it. Smiling is a significant way of bringing joy and peace not only to our own lives but to the lives of the people we are surrounded by. It indicates that we are in control of our lives. Smiling can relax our nervous system and fill us with a sense of inner joy and peace. However, it is not always easy to smile. At times, we really don't feel like smiling – but try to do it anyway, it's good for your health!

> Recently, one friend asked me, 'How can I force myself to smile when I am filled with sorrow? It isn't natural.' I told her she must be able to smile to her sorrow, because we are more than our sorrow. A human being is like a television set with millions of channels . . . If we turn sorrow on, we are sorrow. If we turn a smile on, we really are the smile. We cannot let just one channel dominate us. We have the seed of everything in us, and we have to seize the situation in our hand, to recover our own sovereignty.[25]

Wearing a smile or calling up a pleasant image that can bring about a smile can positively influence our entire system, even if we are feeling sad or negative. It opens and relaxes our face, which leads to comforting our entire body.[26] Furthermore, smiling affects our self-image and all the attitudes and feelings it entails. Smiling also fosters proper movement of blood and energy in the body for healing, and provides for our brain and nervous system to better work with and regulate our internal organs.

Today, the medical field is becoming more cognizant of the therapeutic value of smiling:

> The mere act of smiling repetitively helps to interrupt mood disorders and strengthen the brain's neural ability to maintain a positive outlook on life.[27]

Smiling can also help us move away from our physical and psychological pains:

> Dr. David Bresler, a former director of the pain control unit at the University of California in Los Angeles, encourages his patients to move away from their pain by smiling. He even

writes prescriptions for his patients that direct them to go to the mirror and smile twice an hour.[28]

Smiling helps strengthen the thymus gland, an important contributor to a healthy immune system, because the zygomaticus major (those smile muscles) and the thymus gland are closely linked.[29]

Like laughter, smiling is also contagious. Even faking a smile can lift us up when we feel down and can connect us to others. It has been said that 'A smile costs nothing, but gives much. It enriches those who receive, without making poorer those who give. It takes but a moment, but the memory of it sometimes last forever.'[30]

Train yourself to start the day with a smile. This practice will be an indication of your will to live that day in happiness and peace. One writer suggests hanging a reminder such as a painting or some inspiring words in your window or from the ceiling above your bed so you can notice it when you wake up in the morning.[31] If you practise mantra meditation regularly, an alternate approach is to say your mantra silently in your mind with a smile as you open your eyes in the morning.

Even fake smiles can eventually turn into genuine ones when you gradually learn to appreciate all you have been blessed with in life. Then, those genuine smiles will be outward expressions of inner joy, something much praised in religious texts:

A cheerful heart is a good medicine, but a downcast spirit dries up the bones.[32]

O let us live in joy, in peace amongst those who struggle! Among men who struggle, let us live in peace. O let us live in joy, although having nothing! In joy let us live like spirits of light![33]

Be glad in the Lord, and rejoice, O righteous, and shout for joy, all you upright in heart!³⁴

A glad heart makes a cheerful countenance, but by sorrow of heart the spirit is broken.³⁵

Rejoice in the Lord always; again I will say, rejoice.³⁶

I keep the Lord always before me; because he is at my right hand, I shall not be moved. Therefore my heart is glad, and my soul rejoices; my body also dwells secure . . . Thou dost show me the path of life; in your presence there is fullness of joy; in thy right hand are pleasures forevermore.³⁷

. . . with faces joyous and beaming with light, associate with your neighbour.³⁸

Be worthy of the trust of thy neighbour, and look upon him with a bright and friendly face.³⁹

You must always be happy. You must associate with joyous and happy people and be adorned with divine morals. Happiness has a direct influence in preserving our health while being upset causes illness.⁴⁰

Cleansing the Mirror of the Heart

Burn ye away the veils with the fire of My love, and dispel ye the mists of vain imaginings by the power of this Name through which We have subdued the entire creation.⁴¹

In the course of our daily life, when negative thoughts and emotions arise, we can immediately *turn the mirror of our heart towards God* as a flower turns towards the life-giving rays of the sun. Negative thoughts and emotions usually assail us in the moments when we are forgetful of God. So, in those moments, reach out to Him and repeat your mantra to regain your peace and composure.

A well-known negative emotion is anger, which often arises from stress. Some people believe that venting anger is good for our health because it helps us release built-up tension. However, recent studies seem to indicate that expressing anger could lead to more anger and result in poor mental and physical health. Furthermore, our anger could affect those with whom we come into contact and add to their problems.[42] In the Tablet of Medicine (*Lawḥ-i Ṭibb*), Bahá'u'lláh teaches us to avoid grief, jealousy and anger. On the effect of these negative emotions on our health, He says:

> Yield not to grief and sorrow; they cause the greatest misery. Jealousy consumeth the body and anger doth burn the liver; avoid these two as you would a lion.[43]

Two other negative emotions to which we should not succumb are greed and envy:

> The darkness of greed and envy becloudeth the radiance of the soul even as the clouds obstruct the light of the sun. Should anyone hearken unto this utterance with a discerning ear, he will unfurl the wings of detachment and soar effortlessly in the atmosphere of true understanding.[44]

As Linda Popov notes in her book *The Family Virtues Guide*, 'the moment you envy someone else, you are rejecting the gifts that are yours'.[45]

Next time we feel overwhelmed with envy, jealously, hate or anger, let us remember the advice of 'Abdu'l-Bahá and engage in *cleansing the mirror of our hearts* from these negative emotions, removing 'the dust which prevents reflection of the rays of the Sun of Reality in the mirror'.[46] The short metta meditation session described below may be helpful for this.

Start off by spending a few minutes in either verbal or mental recitation of your mantra, for example the Greatest Name, to *purify the mirror of your heart*. Then, visualize the person for whom you have strong negative emotions and, in your heart and mind, say: *May you be happy. May you be healthy. May all things be well for you.* You can also bring to mind this Hidden Word of Bahá'u'lláh:

> O Friend! In the garden of thy heart plant naught but the rose of love . . . [47]

Continue with the metta meditation for a few minutes until your soul finds rest and peace.

Practising a Day of Positive Thinking

Negative thinking is a destructive habit, but with practice and perseverance it can be overcome and replaced with positive thinking. For starters, set aside a full day for positive thinking. In the course of that day, stay away from saying or thinking about anything that is negative. This may sound very hard at first, but with dedication, discipline and concentration it can be achieved.

Negative thoughts are typically either about ourselves, others, or situations involving us or other people. During your first day of positive thinking, you must be very gentle and forgiving to yourself. You cannot overcome months or years of negativity overnight. As negativity arises in your mind, simply observe it and smile. This simple exercise is very empowering. It gives you the confidence and assurance that it is ultimately you yourself who can decide to be positive or negative about a certain individual or situation.[48] Don't expect a perfect first day. Consider any progress as success and then aim for a second day of positive thinking. Little by little, you can build additional confidence and determination to spend an entire day with less and less negativity. Before you know it, you will have a solid hold over your thoughts, and negative ones will begin to show up less often and with less intensity.

EPILOGUE

19

AN ANGEL FOR THE DAY

The meaning of 'angels' is the confirmations of God and His celestial powers. Likewise angels are blessed beings who have severed all ties with this nether world, have been released from the chains of self and desires of the flesh, and anchored their hearts to the heavenly realms of the Lord. These are of the Kingdom, heavenly; these are of God, spiritual; these are the revealers of God's abounding grace; these are dawning-points of His spiritual bestowals.

'Abdu'l-Bahá [1]

By 'angel' is meant the power of the confirmations of God – that the candle of God's confirming power shineth out from the lamp-niche of those souls – meaning that every one of those beings will be granted the most vehement confirming support.
'Abdu'l-Bahá [2]

The idea that angels can bring blessings to our lives, guide us to the right path, and protect us finds support in the following passages from the Bahá'í Writings, the Qur'án and the Bible:

Ye are the trees of the Garden of My Sanctity which I planted in hallowed grounds with the Hand of Mercy, then watered with the showers of My imperishable grace, and guarded with the aid of protecting angels from the changes and chances of this world. [3]

O Lord! Assist those who have renounced all else but Thee,

and grant them a mighty victory. Send down upon them, O Lord, the concourse of the angels in heaven and earth and all that is between, to aid Thy servants, to succour and strengthen them, to enable them to achieve success, to sustain them, to invest them with glory, to confer upon them honour and exaltation, to enrich them and to make them triumphant with a wondrous triumph.[4]

He it is who bestows His blessings upon you, with His angels so that He might take you out of the depths of darkness into the light.[5]

Each hath a succession of angels before him and behind him, who watch over him by God's behest.[6]

Over every soul is set a guardian.[7]

Because you have made the Lord your refuge, the Most High your habitation, no evil shall befall you . . . For He will give his angels charge of you to guard you in all your ways. On their hands they will bear you up, lest you dash your foot against a stone.[8]

Are they not all ministering spirits sent forth to serve, for the sake of those who are to obtain salvation?[9]

The hosts of the Kingdom will assist (thee) and the heavenly armies will protect and defend thee. Wherefore seek bounties as much as thou canst.[10]

Help them, O my Lord, under all conditions, support them at all times with Thine angels of holiness, they who are Thine invisible hosts, Thy heavenly battalions who bring down to defeat the massed armies of this nether world.[11]

Verily, We behold you from Our realm of glory, and shall

aid whosoever will arise for the triumph of Our Cause with the hosts of the Concourse on high and a company of Our favoured angels.[12]

The Bahá'í Writings teach that we can not only be helped by angels, but have the potential to become angelic ourselves and serve as companions to other angels:

Ye are the angels, if your feet be firm, your spirits rejoiced, your secret thoughts pure, your eyes consoled, your ears opened, your breasts dilated with joy, and your souls gladdened, and if you arise to assist the Covenant, to resist dissension and to be attracted to the Effulgence! Verily, I say unto you that the Word of God has assuredly been explained and has become an evident sign and a strong and solid proof, and its traces shall be spread in the East and West, and to these all heads shall bow and all souls shall submit and kneel down with their faces to the ground.[13]

Endeavour thou to become the true president of the assemblies of spiritual souls, and a companion to the angels in the realm of the All-Merciful.[14]

Array yourselves in the perfection of divine virtues. I hope you may be quickened and vivified by the breaths of the Holy Spirit. Then shall ye indeed become the angels of heaven whom Christ promised would appear in this Day to gather the harvest of divine planting.[15]

I hope that all the friends become manifestors of knowledge and the centres of merciful feelings. Each of them become like unto an angel and radiate heavenly deeds, thoughts and actions.[16]

Prayer, meditation, and reflection on the inner meanings of the Word of God are indispensable to our spiritual development while on earth; so is seeking assistance from angels or holy souls who have passed on from this life:

> If thou be a man of communion and prayer, soar up on the wings of assistance from Holy Souls, that thou mayest behold the mysteries of the Friend and attain to the lights of the Beloved.[17]

If you find the concept of adopting 'an angel for the day' appealing, why not pick your own angels from holy souls who are no longer among us? As a Bahá'í, I have often been inspired by the following individuals whom I call upon in times of difficulty:

- Distinguished Bahá'ís who were my spiritual mentors and who deeply affected me. These include individuals who eventually gave their lives for their beliefs in Iran. For example:
  - Professor 'Alí-Murád Dávoodí (http://www.facebook. com/drdavoodi)
  - Mr Muhammad Movahhed (http://www.facebook. com/muhammadmovahhed)
  - Mr *Badi'u'lláh Faríd* (http://www.facebook.com/ badiullahfarid)
- Renowned Bahá'í figures such as Mírzá Abu'l-Faḍl-i-Gulpáygání, who was not only a foremost Bahá'í scholar but also the only individual of whom 'Abdu'l-Bahá is known to have said 'He is my own self.'[18]
- Early disciples of Bahá'u'lláh whose accounts were recorded by 'Abdu'l-Bahá in *Memorials of the Faithful*. Marzieh Gail, who translated this collection into English, has this to say about the work:

> ... this is more than the brief annals of early Bahá'í disciples; it is somehow, a book of prototypes; and it is a kind of testament of values endorsed and willed to us by the Bahá'í Exemplar ['Abdu'l-Bahá], values now derided, but – if the planet is to be made safe for humanity – indispensable. These are short and

simple accounts, but they constitute a manual of how to live, and how to die.[19]

Regardless of whom you pick as an *angel*, first make sure you develop a good understanding of their lives and deeds. Then, following your morning meditation and contemplation of the Word of God, bring one of them to mind and seek their assistance for the day.

Call them by their names and ask them to pray for you so you can live a God-centred life – a life of humility and selflessness, of courage and devotion, of patience and inner calm; a life occupied with remembrance of God and reliance on Him. Ask them to teach you the art of loving God and being spiritually joyous. Ask them to pray that you may attain to your life's purpose. Ask them to pray for you and for all the people in your life whom you think are in need of prayers. Enlarge the circle and ask for prayers for all who are suffering in this world and for their joy and happiness in all the worlds of God. Below are a few examples of these *angels* from *Memorials of the Faithful*:

Ṭáhirih

In *Memorials of the Faithful*, 'Abdu'l-Bahá describes Ṭáhirih as 'a woman chaste and holy, a sign and token of surpassing beauty, a burning brand of the love of God, a lamp of His bestowal'.[20] Elsewhere He said, 'At the time of the appearance of the Báb she showed such tremendous courage and power that all who heard her were astonished . . . She bore persecution and suffering with the greatest heroism . . .'[21]

Professor E. G. Browne of Cambridge University wrote of her: 'Alike in virtue of her marvellous beauty, her rare intellectual gifts, her fervid eloquence, her fearless devotion, and her glorious martyrdom, she stands incomparable and immortal amidst her countrywomen. Had the religion of the Báb no other claim to greatness, this were sufficient – that it produced a heroine like Qurratu'l-'Ayn [Tahirih].'[22]

Mishkín-Qalam

Mishkín-Qalam was one of the foremost Persian calligraphists of the 19th century. About him, 'Abdu'l-Bahá writes:

> He had no ties to this life, but spent his days and nights supplicating and communing with God. He was always smiling, effervescing; he was spirit personified, love embodied. For sincerity and loyalty he had no match, nor for patience and inner calm. He was selflessness itself, living on the breaths of the spirit.
>
> If he had not been in love with the Blessed Beauty, if he had not set his heart on the Realm of Glory, every worldly pleasure could have been his. Wherever he went, his many calligraphic styles were a substantial capital, and his great accomplishment brought him attention and respect from rich and poor alike. But he was hopelessly enamoured of man's one true Love, and thus he was free of all those other bonds, and could float and soar in the spirit's endless sky.[23]

Shaykh Sádiq-i-Yazdí

> His detachment from the things of this world and his attachment to the life of the spirit are indescribable. He was love embodied, tenderness personified. Day and night, he commemorated God. Utterly unconscious of this world and all that is therein, he dwelt continually on God, remaining submerged in supplications and prayers. Most of the time, tears poured from his eyes. The Blessed Beauty [Bahá'u'lláh] singled him out for special favour, and whenever He turned His attention toward Sádiq, His loving-kindness was clear to see.[24]

Mashhadí Fattáh

> Mashhadí Fattáh was personified spirit . . . He was utter selflessness; from him, no one ever heard a syllable to indicate

that he existed. He was always in a certain corner of the prison, silently meditating, occupied with the remembrance of God; at all times spiritually alert and mindful, in a state of supplication.[25]

Pidar-Ján of Qazvín

He was a godly old man, enamoured of the Well-Beloved; in the garden of Divine love, he was like a rose full-blown. He . . . spent his days and nights communing with God and chanting prayers; and although he walked the earth, he travelled the heights of Heaven.

To obey the law of God, he took up a trade, for he had nothing. He would bundle a few pairs of socks under his arm and peddle them as he wandered through the streets and bázárs, and thieves would rob him of his merchandise. Finally he was obliged to lay the socks across his outstretched palms as he went along. But he would get to chanting a prayer, and one day he was surprised to find that they had stolen the socks, laid out on his two hands, from before his eyes. His awareness of this world was clouded, for he journeyed through another. He dwelt in ecstasy; he was a man drunken, bedazzled.

For some time, that is how he lived in 'Iráq. Almost daily he was admitted to the presence of Bahá'u'lláh. His name was 'Abdu'lláh but the friends bestowed on him the title of Pidar-Ján – Father Dear – for he was a loving father to them all. At last, under the sheltering care of Bahá'u'lláh, he took flight to the 'seat of truth, in the presence of the potent king'.[26]

Departed souls can inspire us. Thus, reaching out to 'angels' could result in guidance and inspiration:

There is no doubt that the forces of the higher worlds interplay with the forces of this plane. The heart of man is open to inspiration; this is spiritual communication.[27]

When you do not know it, and are in a receptive attitude, they [the departed] are able to make suggestions to you, if you are in difficulty.[28]

BIBLIOGRAPHY

'Abdu'l-Bahá. *'Abdu'l-Bahá in London: Addresses and Notes of Conversations*. London: Bahá'í Publishing Trust, 1982.

— *Memorials of the Faithful*. Trans. Marzieh Gail. Wilmette, Ill.: Bahá'í Publishing Trust, 1975.

— *Paris Talks: Addresses Given by 'Abdu'l-Bahá in Paris in 1911*. 12th ed. London: Bahá'í Publishing Trust, 1995.

— *The Secret of Divine Civilization*. Wilmette, Ill.: Bahá'í Publishing Trust, 1979.

— *Selections from the Writings of 'Abdu'l-Bahá*. Haifa: Bahá'í World Centre, 1978.

— *Tablets of Abdul-Baha Abbas*. 3 vols. Chicago: Bahá'í Publishing Society, 1909–1916.

— 'Tablet of the Greatest Name'. Available at: http://bahai-library.com/ abdulbaha_greatest_name.

— *The Promulgation of Universal Peace: Talks Delivered by 'Abdu'l-Baha During His Visit to the United States and Canada in 1912* (1922, 1925). Comp. H. MacNutt. Wilmette, IL: Bahá'í Publishing Trust, 2nd ed. 1982.

'Abu'l-Faḍl, Mírzá. *'Elucidation of the Meaning of "The Greatest Name"*. (with words of 'Abdu'l-Bahá copied by May Maxwell). Available at: http://bahai-library.com/essays/greatestname.fadl.html.

Ajaya, Swami. *Yoga Psychology: A Practical Guide to Meditation*. 3rd ed. Honesdale, Pennsylvania: The Himalayan International Institute of Yoga Science and Philosophy, 1978.

'Attár, Farid al-Din. *Muslim Saints and Mystics: Episodes from the Tadhkirat al-Auliya' (Memorial of the Saints)*. Trans. A. J. Arberry. London: Penguin, 1990.

Báb, The. *Selections from the Writings of the Báb*. Trans. Habib Taherzadeh. Haifa: Bahá'í World Centre, 1978.

Badiei, Amir. *Stories Told by 'Abdu'l-Bahá*. Oxford: George Ronald, 2007.

Bahá'í Prayers: A Selection of Prayers. Wilmette, Ill.: Bahá'í Publishing Trust, 2002.

Bahá'u'lláh. *Ad'íyiy-i-Ḥaḍrat-i Maḥbúb,* Cairo, 1921.

— *Epistle to the Son of the Wolf.* Trans. Shoghi Effendi. Wilmette, Ill.: Bahá'í Publishing Trust, 1976.

— *Gems of Divine Mysteries: Javáhiru'l-Asrár.* Haifa: Bahá'í World Centre, 2002.

— *Gleanings from the Writings of Bahá'u'lláh.* Trans. Shoghi Effendi. 2nd ed. Wilmette, Ill.: Bahá'í Publishing Trust, 1983.

— *The Hidden Words of Bahá'u'lláh.* Bundoora, Melbourne: Century Press, 2005.

— *The Kitáb-i-Aqdas: The Most Holy Book.* Haifa: Bahá'í World Centre, 1992.

— *Majmú'iy-i-Alváḥ* (A Collection of Tablets of Bahá'u'lláh). Cairo, 1920.

— *Prayers and Meditations by Bahá'u'lláh.* Trans. Shoghi Effendi. Wilmette, Ill.: Bahá'í Publishing Trust, 1987.

— *The Seven Valleys And The Four Valleys.* Trans. Marzieh Gail. Wilmette, Ill.: Bahá'í Publishing Trust, 1978.

— *The Summons of the Lord of Hosts: Tablets of Bahá'u'lláh.* Haifa, Israel: Bahá'í World Centre, 2002.

— *The Tabernacle of Unity: Bahá'u'lláh's Responses to Manikchi Sahib and Other Writings.* Haifa: Bahá'í World Centre, 2006.

— 'Tablet of All Food'. Provisional translation by Stephen Lambden. Available at: http://bahai-library.com/provisionals/food.html.

— *Tablets of Bahá'u'lláh Revealed after the Kitáb-i-Aqdas.* Trans. Habib Taherzadeh. Haifa: Bahá'í World Centre, 1978.

— 'Tablet of Medicine' (Tablet to a Physician). Provisional translation by Khazeh Fananapazir and Stephen Lambden: 'Tablet of Medicine: Lawḥ-i-Ṭibb', in *Bahá'í Studies Bulletin,* vol. 6, nos. 4–7:2 (1992), pp. 18–65. Available at: http://bahai-library.com/wwwboard/messageso2/157.html.

Barbor, Cary. 'The Science of Meditation', in *Psychology Today,* May/June 2001. Available at: http://www.psychologytoday.com/articles/200105/the-science-meditation.

Begley, Sharon. 'The Lotus and the Synapse', in *The Daily Beast,* 25 May 2008. Available at: http://www.thedailybeast.com/newsweek/blogs/lab-notes/2008/03/25/the-lotus-and-the-synapse.html.

Benson, Herbert. 'Mind-Body Pioneer', in *Psychology Today,* 1 May 2001. Available at: http://www.psychologytoday.com/articles/200105/mind-body-pioneer.

— *The Relaxation Response*. New York: Avon Books, 1974.

The Bhagavad Gita. Trans. Juan Mascaro. London: Penguin Books, 1988.

Bible. Revised Standard Version. New York: Thomas Nelson & Sons, 1952; Authorized King James Version. Grand Rapids, MI: Zondervan, 1983.

Blumenfeld, Larry. *The Big Book of Relaxation: Simple Techniques to Control the Excess Stress in Your Life*. Roslyn, NY: The Relaxation Company, 1994.

Brantly, Jeffrey; Millstine, Wendy. *Five Good Minutes in the Evening: 100 Mindful Practices to Help Unwind from the Day and Make the Most of Your Night*. Oakland, CA: New Harbinger, 2006.

Breakwell, Thomas; Brittingham, Isabella; Hopper, Herbert. *Utterances of Our Blessed Master, 'Abdu'l-Bahá, in His Exact Words, Revealed to Three Pilgrims; Thomas Breakwell of England, Herbert Hopper (an American) from Paris, and Isabella D. Brittingham of America, September, 1901.* Available at: http://bahai-library.com/breakwell_hopper_brittingham.

Breathnach, Sarah Ban. *The Simple Abundance: Journal of Gratitude*. New York: Warner Books, 1996.

Brent, Bill. *Holy Silence: The Gift of Quaker Spirituality*. Brewster, MA: Paraclete, 2005.

Cahn, B. R.; Polich, J. 'Meditation States and Traits: EEG, ERP, and Neuroimaging Studies', in *Psychological Bulletin*, vol. 132, no. 2 (2006), pp. 180–211. doi:10.1037/0033-2909.132.2.180. PMID 16536641.

Carnegie, Dale. *How to Stop Worrying and Start Living: Time Tested Methods for Conquering Worry*. New York: Pocket Books, 1984.

Carr, L; Iacoboni, M; Dubeau, M.C; Mazziotta, J.C; Lenzi, G.L. 'Neural Mechanisms of Empathy in Humans: A Relay from Neural Systems for Imitation to Limbic Areas', in *Proceedings of the National Academy of Science*, vol. 100, no. 9 (2003), pp. 5497–5502. Available at: http://www.pnas.org/content/100/9/5497.abstract?ijkey=6640cf097 0746ca12715deofbf4ba6651660f156&keytype2=tf_ipsecsha.

Carrington, Patricia. *The Book of Meditation: The Complete Guide to Modern Meditation*. Boston, MA: Element, 1998.

Chang, Larry (comp.). *Wisdom for the Soul: Five Millennia of Prescriptions for Spiritual Healing*. Washington DC: Gnosophia, 2006.

The Cloud of Unknowing: The Classic of Medieval Mysticism. Ed. Evelyn Underhill (1922). Mineola, NY: Dover, 2003.

The Compilation of Compilations. Prepared by the Universal House of Justice 1963–1990. 2 vols. Sydney: Bahá'í Publications Australia, 1991.

Dass, Ram. *Journey of Awakening: A Meditator's Guidebook*. New York: Bantam, 1978.

Davidson,R. J. et al. 'Long-term Meditators Self-induce High-amplitude Gamma Synchrony During Mental Practice'. Available at: http://www.ncbi.nlm.nih.gov/pmc/articles/PMC526201/?tool=pubmed.

— 'Neural Correlates of Attentional Expertise in Long-term Meditation Practitioners'. Available at: http://www.ncbi.nlm.nih.gov/pmc/articles/PMC1903340/?tool=pubmed.

— 'Regulation of the Neural Circuitry of Emotion by Compassion Meditation: Effects of Meditative Expertise'. Available at: http://www.plosone.org/article/info:doi/10.1371/journal.pone.0001897.

Davis, Avram (ed.). *Meditation from the Heart of Judaism: Today's Teachers Share Their Practices, Techniques*. Woodstock, VT: Jewish Lights Publishing, 1997.

Davich, Victor. *The Best Guide to Meditation*. New York: St. Martin's Griffin, 1998.

Decety, J.; Chaminade, T. 'Neural Correlates of Feeling Sympathy', in *Neuropsychologia*, vol. 41, no. 2 (2003), pp. 127–138.

— et al. 'Who Caused the Pain? An fMRI Investigation of Empathy and Intentionality in Children', in *Neuropsychologia*, vol. 46 (2008), pp. 2607–2614. Available at: http://chicago.academia.edu/KalinaMichalska/Papers/111455/Who_caused_the_pain_An_fMRI_investigation_of_empathy_and_intentionality_in_children.

De Mello, Anthony. *Contact with God*. New York: Image Doubleday, 2003.

Dennis, Chernin. *How to Meditate Using Chakras, Mantras, and Breath*. Ann Arbor, MI: Think Publication, 2002.

Deshpande, M. S. (ed.). *The Way to God: Selected Writings from Mahatma Gandhi*. Berkeley: North Atlantic Books, 2009.

Devananda, Swami Vishnu. *Meditation and Mantras*. New York: OM Lotus Publishing, 1978.

The Dhammapada: The Path to Perfection. Trans. Juan Mascaro. London: Penguin Books, 1988.

Easwaran, Eknath. *The Mantram Handbook*. Tomales, CA: Nilgiri Press, 1998.

Emmons, Robert. *Thanks! How the New Science of Gratitude Can Make You Happier*. Boston: Houghton Mifflin, 2007.

Fraser, Andy. 'They thought something was wrong with the machine', in *The View: The Rigpa Journal*, August 2009. Available at: http://www.viewmagazine.org/index.php/articles/science/103--they-thought-something-was-wrong-with-the-machine.html.

Gandhi, Mohandas K. *Prayer.* Ed. John Strobmeier. Berkeley, CA: Berkeley Hills Books, 2000.

— *Ramanama.* Ahmedabad: Navajivan, 1949.

Gawain, Shakti. *Creative Visualization.* New York: Bantam, 1982.

Gawler, Ian. *Peace of Mind: How You Can Learn to Meditate and Use the Power of Your Mind.* New York: Garden City Park, 1989.

Gillet, Lev. *On the Invocation of the Name of Jesus.* Springfield, Ill.: Templegate, 1985.

Goleman, Daniel. *The Meditative Mind: The Varieties of Meditative Experiences.* New York: G.P. Putnam's Sons, 1988.

Griffith, Ralph T. H. *Hymns of the Rigveda.* Benares: Medical Hall Press, 1926.

Hanh, Thich Nhat. *Being Peace.* Berkeley, CA: Parallax Press, 1987.

— *The Miracle of Mindfulness.* Boston: Beacon Press, 1987.

— *Peace Is Every Step: The Path of Mindfulness in Everyday Life.* London: Bantam, 1992.

Harvey, John. *The Quiet Mind.* Honesdale, PA: Himalayan International Institute of Yoga and Philosophy, 1988.

Helminski, Camille. *Women of Sufism: A Hidden Treasure.* Boston, Massachusetts: Shambhala, 2003.

'History of Meditation: East and West'. Available at: http://web.archive.org/web/20090603084443/http://www.altmd.com/Articles/History-of-Meditation.

Holden, Janice Miner; Greyson, Bruce; James, Debbie. *The Handbook of Near-Death Experience: Thirty Years of Investigation.* Santa Barbara, CA: Praeger, 2009.

Honnold, Annamarie. *Vignettes from the Life of 'Abdu'l-Bahá.* Oxford: George Ronald, 2006.

Immordino-Yang, Mary H. et al. 'Neural Correlates of Admiration and Compassion' in *Proceedings of the National Academy of Sciences of the United States of America*, March 2009. Available at: http://www.pnas.org/content/106/19/8021.full.

Jacobs, Gregg. *Say Goodnight To Insomnia.* New York: Henry Holt, 1999.

Kabat-Zinn, Jon. *Full Catastrophe Living: Using the Wisdom of Your Body and Mind to Face Stress, Pain, and Illness.* New York: Delacorte Press, 1990.

Kabbani, Shaykh Muhammad Hisham. *The Naqshbandi Sufi Tradition Guidebook of Daily Practices and Devotions.* Washington, DC: Islamic Supreme Council of America, 2004.

Kaplan, Aryeh. *Jewish Meditation: A Practical Guide*. New York: Schocken Books, 1985.

Klein, Allen. *The Healing Power of Humor: Techniques for Getting Through Loss, Setbacks, Upsets, Disappointments, Difficulties, Trials, Tribulations, and All That Not-So-Funny Stuff*. New York: G.P. Putnam's Sons, 1989.

Lambden, Stephen. 'The Du 'a Saḥār or Supplication of Glory-Beauty (al-bahā) (Ramaḍān Dawn Prayer) of Imam Muhammad al-Bāqir', University of Newcastle upon Tyne, 2002, rev. Ohio 2007. Available at: http://www.hurqalya.pwp.blueyonder.co.uk/03-Biblical-islam-BBst/dawnP.htm.

— 'Greatest Name, The (al-Ism al-A'zam)', article for possible inclusion in *Bahá'í Encyclopedia*, 1995. Available at: http://bahai-library.com/lambden_encyclopedia_greatest_name.

— 'The Word Bahá: Quintessence of the Greatest Name', in *Bahá'í Studies Review*, vol. 3, no. 1 (1993). Available at: http://bahai-library.com/bsr/bsr03_1/312_lambden_baha.htm.

Lawrence, of the Resurrection brother. *The Practice of the Presence of God with Spiritual Maxims*. Old Tappan, NJ: Fleming H. Revell, 1967.

Leloup, Jean-Yves. *Being Still: Reflections on an Ancient Mystical Tradition*. New York: Paulist Press, 1990.

LeShan, Lawrence. *How to Meditate: A Guide to Self-Discovery*. New York: Little Brown, 1974.

Levey, Joel; Levey, Michelle. *Simple Meditation and Relaxation*. California: Conari Press, 1999.

Lewis, Dennis. *Free Your Breath, Free Your Life: How Conscious Breathing Can Relieve Stress, Increase Vitality, and Help You Live More Fully*. Boston, MA: Shambhala, 2004.

Lights of Guidance: A Bahá'í Reference File. Comp. Helen Hornby. New Delhi: Bahá'í Publishing Trust, 1983.

Lucas, Mary L. *A Brief Account of My Visit to Acca*. Chicago, Ill.: Bahá'í Publishing Society, 1905.

Makarios, Saint Metropolitan of Corinth; The Hagiorite Saint Nicodemus. *Writings from the Philokalia on Prayer of the Heart*. Trans. from the original Russian text *Dobrotolubiye* by E. Kadloubovsky and G.E.H. Palmer. London: Faber and Faber, 1951.

Masumian, Farnaz. *A Study of the Afterlife in World Religions*. Los Angeles, CA: Kalimát Press, 2002.

— ; Masumian, Bijan. *Divine Educators*. Oxford: George Ronald, 2005.

Mataji, Vandana. *Nama Japa: The Prayer of the Name*. New Delhi: Motilal Banarsidass, 1997.

Maxwell, May. *An Early Pilgrimage*. Oxford: George Ronald, 1953, 1969.

Michaelson, Jay. *God in Your Body : Kabbalah, Mindfulness and Embodied Spiritual Practice*. Woodstock, VT: Jewish Lights Publication, 2007.

Miskiman, D. E. 'The Treatment of Insomnia by the Transcendental Meditation Program', in *Scientific Research on the Transcendental Meditation Program: Collected Papers*, ed. D. W. Orme-Johnson and J. T. Farrow, vol. I, pp. 296–300. Livingston Manor, NY: Maharishi European Research University Press, 1978.

Moen, Larry. *Meditations for Healing*. Lithia Springs, Georgia: New Leaf, 1998.

Momen, Moojan. *Buddhism and the Bahá'í Faith: An Introduction to the Bahá'í Faith for Theravada Buddhists*. Oxford: George Ronald, 1995.

— 'The Concept of Light in Iranian Religion', Conference Presentation, Lectures in Bahá'í Studies, Department of Middle Eastern History, University of Haifa, Israel, 25 March 2003.

Momen, Wendi. *Meditation*. Oxford: George Ronald, 1996.

Moody, A. R. Jr. *Life After Life: The Investigation of a Phenomenon – Survival of Bodily Death*. Harrisburg, PA: Stackpole Books, 1976.

Mu'ayyad, Ḥabíb. *Kháṭirát-i-Ḥabíb* (Memoirs of Habib), vol. 1. Tehran, 1961.

Naqshbandi Sufi Order of America. 'Dhikr: Remembrance of God'. Available at: http://www.naqshbandi.org/topics/dhikr.htm.

Nawawi. *An-Nawawi's Forty Hadith: An Anthology of the Prophet Muhammad*. Trans. Ibrahim Ezzeddin and Denys Johnson-Davies (Abdul Wadoud). Cambridge: Islamic Text Society, 1997.

Newberg, Andrew; Waldman, Mark. *How God Changes Your Brain: Breakthrough Findings from a Leading Neuroscientist*. New York: Ballantine Books, 2009.

Orme-Johnson, D. W. 'Medical Care Utilization and the Transcendental Meditation Program', in *Psychosomatic Medicine*, no. 49 (1987), pp. 493–507.

'Pennsylvania Man Buried with his Beloved Corvette'. The History Channel, n.d. Available at www.History.com.

Pinson, DovBer. *Meditation and Judaism: Exploring the Jewish Meditative Paths*. Lanham, Maryland: Rowman and Littlefield, 2004.

Piver, Susan (ed. and comp.). *Quiet Mind: A Beginner's Guide to Meditation*. Boston, MA: Shambhala, 2008.

Popov, Linda Kavelin. *The Family Virtues Guide: Simple Ways to Bring Out the Best in Our Children and Ourselves*. New York: Plume, 1997.

Profaska, Paul. *Calm Handbook: A Communal Approach to Learning*

Meditation. Oxford: George Ronald, 2005.

Qur'án. *The Message of the Quran,* trans. and explained by Muhammad Asad. Gibraltar, 1980; *The Koran,* trans. J. M. Rodwell (1909). New York: Dutton, 1971.

Rama, Swami. *Meditation and Its Practice.* Honesdale, PA: Himalayan Institute Press, 2005.

Reininger, Gustave. *Centering Prayer in Daily Life and Ministry.* New York: Continuum, 1998.

Rimé Foundation. 'Preserving the Past, Enlightening the Present'. Available at: http://rimefoundation.org/ymro9.php.

Roche, Lorin. *Whole Body Meditations: Igniting Your Natural Instinct to Heal.* Emmaus, PA: Rodale Books, 2002.

Rosenberg, Larry, with David Guy. *Breath by Breath: The Liberating Practice of Insight Meditation.* Boston, MA: Shambhala, 1998.

Salzberg, Sharon. *Loving-kindness: The Revolutionary Art of Happiness.* Boston, MA: Shambhala, 1997.

Samuels, Mike; Samuels, Nancy. *Healing with the Mind's Eye: A Guide to Using Imagery and Visions for Personal Growth and Healing.* New York: Summit Books, 1990.

Sanders, Tim. *Today We Are Rich: Harnessing the Power of Total Confidence.* Carol Stream, Ill.: Tyndale House, 2011.

Saarela, Miiamaaria V. 'The Compassionate Brain: Humans Detect Intensity of Pain from Another's Face', in *Cerebral Cortex,* vol. 17, Issue 1, pp. 230–237. Available at: http://cercor.oxfordjournals.org/content/17/1/230.full.

Scholl, Steven. 'Remembrance of God: An Invocation Technique in Sufism and the Writings of the Báb and Bahá'u'lláh', in *Bahá'í Studies Bulletin,* vol. 2, no. 3 (1983). Available at: http://www.bahaistudies.net/asma/remembranceofgod.pdf.

Shapiro, Eddie; Shapiro, Debbie. *The Meditation Book.* New York: Godsfield Books, 2000.

— *Peace Within the Stillness: Relaxation and Meditation for True Happiness.* Freedom, CA: The Crossing Press, 1998.

— *Meditation for Inner Peace: Your Guide to Relaxation and True Happiness.* London: Piatkus, 2000.

Shoghi Effendi. *Extracts from the Guardian's Letters on Spiritualism, Reincarnation and Related Subjects,* compilation by the Research Department of the Universal House of Justice, February 1970.

— *Letters from the Guardian to Australia and New Zealand 1923–1957.* Sydney: National Spiritual Assembly of the Bahá'ís of Australia, 1970.

— *Principles of Bahá'í Administration: A Compilation*. London: Bahá'í Publishing Trust, 1976.

Singer, Richard. *Eastern Wisdom for Your Soul: 111 Meditations for Everyday Enlightenment*. Dreamriver Press, 2006.

Stein, Joel. 'Just Say Om!', in *Time Magazine*, 4 August 2002. Available at: http://www.time.com/time/magazine/article/0,9171,1005349,00.html.

Stockman, Robert; Winters, Jonah. *A Resource Guide for the Scholarly Study of the Bahá'í Faith*. Wilmette, Ill.: Research Office, US Baha'i National Center.

Stone, Austin J. *The Joy of Meditation: An Introduction to Meditation Techniques*. New York: Square One, 2002.

Thera, Nyanasatta (trans.). *The Foundations of Mindfulness: Satipatthana Sutta*. Kandi, Sri Lanka: Buddhist Publication Society, 1994. Available at: http://www.accesstoinsight.org/lib/authors/nyanasatta/wheel019.html.

Thondup, Tulku. *Boundless Healing: Meditation Exercises to Enlighten the Mind and Heal the Body*. Boston, MA: Shambhala, 2000.

— *The Healing Power of Mind: Simple Meditation Exercises for Health, Well-Being and Enlightenment*. Boston, MA: Shambhala, 1996.

The Three Year Plan. Wilmette, Ill: National Teaching Committee of the Bahá'ís of the United States, 1993.

Upton, Charles (trans.). *Doorkeeper of the Heart: Versions of Rabi'a*. Threshold Sufi Classics, 1988.

Walsh, Roger. *Essential Spirituality: Exercises from the World's Religions to Cultivate Kindness, Love, Joy, Peace, Vision, Wisdom, and Generosity*. Toronto,: John Wiley & Sons, 1999.

Webster, Richard. *Creative Visualization for Beginners: Achieve Your Goals and Make Your Dreams Come True*. Woodbury, Minnesota: Llewellyn Worldwide, 2005.

Wilson, Andrew (ed). *World Scripture: A Comparative Anthology of Sacred Texts*. New York: Paragon House, 1995.

Zarqání, Mírzá Maḥmúd. *Maḥmúd's Diary: The Diary of Mírzá Maḥmúd Zarqání Chronicling 'Abdu'l-Bahá's Journey to America*. Trans. Mohi Sobhani with the assistance of Shirley Macias. Oxford: George Ronald, 1998.

— *Kitáb-i-Badáyi'u'l-Ath*ár. Diary of 'Abdu'l-Bahá's travels to the West, vol. 2. Frankfurt: Bahá'í-Verlag, 1987.

NOTES AND REFERENCES

Preface

1. Quoted in Chang, *Wisdom for the Soul*, p. 243.
2. See 'History of Meditation: East and West'.
3. ibid.
4. fMRI is a specialized type of MRI used to scan and capture brain activity by following changes in the blood flow. Regular MRI is used to study the anatomy of the brain. Think of MRI as a still camera and fMRI as a video camera that captures movement or activity.
5. EEG equipment measures voltage fluctuations or electrical activity within the neurons of the brain along the scalp.
6. See, for example, Cahn and Polich, 'Meditation States and Traits: EEG, ERP, and Neuroimaging Studies'.
7. Benson, *The Relaxation Response*, pp. x-xi.

Part 1

1. Levey and Levey, *Simple Meditation and Relaxation*, p. 26.
2. Quoted ibid. p. 8.
3. ibid. p. ix.

1 Introduction

1. See the case of a former beauty queen who died of complications from a procedure to enlarge her buttocks, at http://abcnews.go.com/Health/Cosmetic/miss-argentinas-death-shows-dangers-buttock-injections/story?id=9221615.
2. 'Pennsylvania man buried with his beloved Corvette', available at: http://www.history.com/this-day-in-history/pennsylvania-man-buried-with-his-beloved-corvette (30 April 2011).
3. Bahá'u'lláh, *Hidden Words*, Arabic no. 59.
4. Bhagavad Gita 18:62.
5. Psalms 73:26.
6. *Hadith:* Arabic, literally 'tradition'; secondary to the Qur'án, hadith

are considered by most Muslims a source of guidance; they refer to
the words or deeds attributed to the Prophet Muhammad.
7. http://www.ezsoftech.com/stories/love.in.islam.asp.
8. *Zikr* or *dhikr*: Arabic, literally 'mention' or 'remembrance' of God.
9. *Mantra* or *mantram*: Sanskrit, literally 'speech or instrument of
thought'.
10. Bahá'u'lláh, *The Seven Valleys and the Four Valleys*, p. 54.
11. 'Abdu'l-Bahá, *Tablets of Abdul-Baha Abbas*, p. 709.
12. Bahá'u'lláh, *Gleanings from the Writings of Bahá'u'lláh*, CLIII, p.
326.

2 What is Meditation?

1. Mataji, *Nama Japa*, p. 53.
2. Harvey, *The Quiet Mind*, p. 18.
3. Momen, *Meditation*, p. 13.
4. LeShan, *How to Meditate*, p. 150.
5. ibid.
6. Kaplan, *Jewish Meditation*, p. 8.
7. ibid. p. 14.
8. Dhammapada 3:36.
9. Pinson, *Meditation and Judaism*, p. 21.
10. Shapiro and Shapiro, *Meditation for Inner Peace*, p. 114.
11. Ajaya, *Yoga Psychology*, p. 10.
12. Levey and Levey, *Simple Meditation and Relaxation*, p. 26.

3 Meditation and the Bahá'í Faith

1. 'Abdu'l-Bahá, *Paris Talks*, no. 54, p. 187.
2. 'Abdu'l-Bahá, *The Promulgation of Universal Peace*, p. 148.
3. Letter on behalf of Shoghi Effendi to an individual believer, in
Bahá'í News, no. 102 (August 1936), p. 3. Available at: http://
bahai-library.com/compilations/prayer.meditation.html.
4. The Universal House of Justice, 'Message Introducing the Three
Year Plan', in *The Three Year Plan*, p. 5.
5. 'Abdu'l-Bahá, *The Promulgation of Universal Peace*, p. 244.
6. ibid. pp. 147–8.
7. Bahá'u'lláh, *Gleanings from the Writings of Bahá'u'lláh*, XXVII, pp.
65–6.
8. 'Abdu'l-Bahá, *Selections from the Writings of 'Abdu'l-Bahá*, no. 73,
pp. 110–11.
9. Mírzá Abu'l-Faḍl, 'Elucidation of the Meaning of "The Greatest
Name"'.
10. Profaska, *Calm Handbook: A Communal Approach to Learning Meditation*, p. 38.

11. ibid.
12. Prov. 18:10.
13. Kabbani, *The Naqshbandi Sufi Tradition*, p. 52.
14. Bahá'u'lláh, *Prayers and Meditations*, CXXVI, p. 213.
15. 'Abdu'l-Bahá, in *United States Supplement to Bahá'í News*, no. 80 (October 1964), p. 2; in *Lights of Guidance*, p. 211.
16. *Bahá'í Prayers*, p. 145.
17. 'Abdu'l-Bahá, 'Tablet of the Greatest Name'.
18. Bahá'u'lláh, *Kitáb-i-Aqdas*, para. 132.
19. Bahá'u'lláh, *Hidden Words*, Persian no. 72.
20. Shoghi Effendi, *Principles of Bahá'í Administration*, p. 10.
21. Letter on behalf of Shoghi Effendi to an individual believer, 19 November 1945, ibid.
22. Stockman and Winters, *A Resource Guide for the Scholarly Study of the Bahá'í Faith*, p. 91.
23. Letter on behalf of Shoghi Effendi to an individual believer, 25 January 1943, in *Spiritual Foundations: Prayer, Meditation, and the Devotional Attitude*, no. 50.
24. Letter on behalf of Shoghi Effendi to an individual believer, 20 November 1937, ibid. no. 45.
25. Bahá'u'lláh, *Gleanings from the Writings of Bahá'u'lláh*, CXVII, p. 250.

4 The Scientific Evidence

1. Benson, 'Mind-Body Pioneer'.
2. Harvey, *Quiet Mind*, pp. 144–6.
3. Bhagavad Gita 6:35.
4. Gawler, *Peace of Mind: How You Can Learn to Meditate and Use the Power of Your Mind*, pp. 22–4.
5. Benson, *The Relaxation Response*, p. xviii.
6. Gawler, *Peace of Mind*, p. 31.
7. Dhammapada 3:43.
8. Roche, *Whole Body Meditations: Igniting Your Natural Instinct to Heal*, pp. x–xi.
9. Thondup, *Boundless Healing: Meditation Exercises to Enlighten the Mind and Heal the Body*.
10. Stein, 'Just Say Om!'
11. Roche, *Whole Body Meditations*, pp. x–xi.
12. Available at: http://www.tmeducation.org/research-national-institutes-of-health.
13. Goleman, *The Meditative Mind*, p. 168.
14. Newberg and Waldman, *How God Changes Your Brain*, p. 191.
15. Roche, *Whole Body Meditations*, p. 5.

16. Orme-Johnson, 'Medical Care Utilization and the Transcendental Meditation Program'.
17. Jacobs, *Say Goodnight to Insomnia*.
18. Miskiman, 'The Treatment of Insomnia by the Transcendental Meditation Program', pp. 296–300.
19. Carrington, *The Book of Meditation: The Complete Guide to Modern Meditation*, pp. 198-9.
20. Barbor, 'The Science of Meditation'.
21. Blumenfeld, *The Big Book of Relaxation*, p. 9.
22. Newberg and Waldman, *How God Changes Your Brain*, p. 191.
23. ibid.
24. Tim Sanders, American author, public speaker, and former Yahoo executive coined this. My husband first heard Tim mention the concept in a keynote speech Tim made at an e-learning conference in Florida in 2010.
25. Newberg and Waldman, *How God Changes Your Brain*, p. 56.
26. Dennis, *How to Meditate Using Chakras, Mantras, and Breath*, pp. 47-8.
27. Blumenfeld, *The Big Book of Relaxation*, p. 9.
28. From the website Holistic-online.com. Available at: http://1stholistic.com/meditation/hol_meditation_benefits_health_spiritual.htm.
29. Newberg and Waldman, *How God Changes Your Brain*, pp. 54-5.
30. ibid. pp. 19-20.
31. Dalai Lama: literally 'Ocean of Wisdom' ; he is the Head of State and spiritual leader of Tibet. The Dalai Lama's followers consider him a Bodhisattva (an enlightened being who, out of compassion, forgos nirvana to save others).
32. Neuroplasticity is a general term referring to the ability of the brain and nervous system in different species to transform themselves structurally and functionally through interaction with the environment. Neuroplasticity can result in the growth of new connections or the creation of new neurons. This can happen while learning any new skill, including meditation. While neuroplasticity is a new term, the idea that the structure of human brain can change with experience is nothing new. See http://mindhacks.com/2010/07/06/neuroplasticity-is-not-a-new-discovery/.
33. Begley, 'The Lotus and the Synapse'.
34. Davidson et al., 'Neural Correlates of Attentional Expertise in Long-term Meditation Practitioners'.
35. Beta, Alpha, Theta, and Delta waves were identified in the 1930s and 1940s. Gamma waves were discovered in the 1960s. They play an important role in harmonizing the various thoughts processed in different parts of the brain.

36. Davidson et al., 'Long-term Meditators Self-induce High-amplitude Gamma Synchrony during Mental Practice'.
37. Davidson et al., 'Regulation of the Neural Circuitry of Emotion by Compassion Meditation: Effects of Meditative Expertise'.
38. Begley, 'The Lotus and the Synapse'.
39. ibid.
40. Decety and Chaminade, 'Neural Correlates of Feeling Sympathy', pp. 127–38.
41. Carr et al., 'Neural Mechanisms of Empathy in Humans: A Relay from Neural Systems for Imitation to Limbic Areas'.
42. Saarela, 'The Compassionate Brain: Humans Detect Intensity of Pain from Another's Face'.
43. Immordino-Yang et al., 'Neural Correlates of Admiration and Compassion'.
44. Decety et al., 'Who Caused the Pain? An fMRI Investigation of Empathy and Intentionality in Children'.
45. Begley, 'The Lotus and the Synapse'.
46. Rimé Foundation, *Preserving the Past, Enlightening the Present*.
47. Fraser, 'They thought something was wrong with the machine'. I would like to thank Dr Ron Manzanero for sending me this article.
48. ibid.
49. ibid.
50. ibid.
51 Thondup, *Boundless Healing*, p. 65.

5 Getting Ready to Meditate

1. The suggestions presented here are based on my personal experiences. They should not be considered prescriptions from the Bahá'í Writings.
2. Davis, *Meditation from the Heart of Judaism*, p. 126.
3. Kabat-Zinn, *Full Catastrophe Living: Using the Wisdom of Your Body and Mind to Face Stress, Pain, and Illness*, p. 68.
4. Shapiro and Shapiro, *Peace Within the Stillness*, p. 46.
5. Rama, *Meditation and Its Practice*, p. 8.
6. Blumenfeld, *The Big Book of Relaxation*, p. 12.
7. Shapiro and Shapiro, *The Meditation Book*, p. 57.
8. Harvey, *The Quiet Mind*, p. 147.
9. Roche, *Whole Body Meditations*, p. 126.
10. Bhagavad Gita 6:35.
11. Shapiro and Shapiro, *The Meditation Book*, p. 50.
12. Ajaya, *Yoga Psychology*, p. 28.
13. Newberg and Waldman, *How God Changes Your Brain*, p. 38.
14. ibid. p. 51.

15. Psalms 46:10.
16. Quoted in Brent, *Holy Silence*, p. 16.
17. ibid.
18. ibid. p. 17.
19. Quoted in Deshpande (ed.), *The Way to God*, p. 54.
20. Dass, *Journey of Awakening*, p. 111.
21. Dhammapada 15:205.
22. Bahá'u'lláh, *Kitáb-i-Aqdas*, para. 115, p. 61.
23. 'Abdu'l-Bahá, *Paris Talks*, p. 186.

Part II

1. Kabat-Zinn, *Full Catastrophe Living*, p. 21.

6 Single Object Meditation

1. Shapiro and Shapiro, The Meditation Book, p. 27.

7 Anapanasati ('Breath Awareness') and Vipassana ('Insight') Meditation

1. Piver, *Quiet Mind*, p. 33.
2. Quoted in Michaelson, *God in Your Body*, p. 38.
3. Piver, *Quiet Mind*, pp. 34–6.
4. Rosenberg, *Breath by Breath*, p. 22.
5. Rosenberg, 'Vipassana : The Practice of Clear Seeing', in Piver, *Quiet Mind*, p. 39.

8 Mindfulness of the Present Moment

1. Quoted in Singer, *Eastern Wisdom for Your Soul*, p. 35.
2. Carnegie, *How to Stop Worry and Start Living*, p. 11.
3. ibid.
4. ibid. p. 33.
5. Levey and Levey, *Simple Meditation and Relaxation*, p. 94.
6. Thera (trans.), *The Foundations of Mindfulness: Satipatthana Sutta*, p. 9.
7. Singer, *Eastern Wisdom for Your Soul*, p. 25.
8. Shapiro and Shapiro, *Peace Within the Stillness*, p. 117.
9. Hanh, *Peace is Every Step: The Path of Mindfulness in Everyday Life*, pp. 42–3.
10. Davich, *The Best Guide to Meditation*, pp. 238–9.
11. Levey and Levey, *Simple Meditation and Relaxation*, pp. 124–5.
12. Thondup, *The Healing Power of Mind*, p. 153.
13. ibid. p. 151.
14. ibid. p. 153.
15. Brantly and Millstine, *Five Good Minutes in the Evening*, pp. 148–9.

16. Hanh, *The Miracle of Mindfulness*, pp. 27–31.
17. Walsh, *Essential Spirituality*, pp. 158–9.
18. ibid.

9 Mindfulness of God: Practising the Presence of God

1. Bahá'u'lláh, *Prayers and Meditations*, X, p. 13.
2. ibid. LV, p. 78.
3. Psalms 16:11.
4. Bahá'u'lláh, *Gleanings*, CXXXIV, p. 290.
5. Qur'án 3:200.
6. ibid. 7:26.
7. ibid. 49:13.
8. Bhagavad Gita 2:72.
9. ibid. 8:7.
10. ibid, 8:8.
11. Qur'án 10:62–4.
12. Nawawi, *An-Nawawi's Forty Hadith*, p. 30.
13. ibid. p. 68.
14. ibid.
15. Bahá'u'lláh, *Gems of Divine Mysteries*, p. 59.
16. Quoted in Badiei, *Stories Told by 'Abdu'l-Bahá*, pp. 80–81; translated and adapted from Mu'ayyad, *Khátirát-i-Habíb*, vol. 1, p. 28.
17. Lawrence, *The Practice of the Presence of God*, p. 25.
18. ibid. p. 27.
19. ibid. pp. 28–9.
20. ibid. pp. 31–3.
21. ibid. pp. 36–45.
22. ibid. p. 46.
23. ibid. pp. 52–9.
24. In 'Attár, *Muslim Saints and Mystics* (trans. Arberry), p. 51.
25. Upton (trans.), *Doorkeeper of the Heart: Versions of Rabi' a.*
26. ibid. p. 44.
27. ibid. p. 46.
28. 'Abdu'l-Bahá, *Memorials of the Faithful*, pp. 84–5.
29. Maxwell, *An Early Pilgrimage*, pp. 20–21.
30. Breakwell, Brittingham and Hopper, *Utterances of our Blessed Master* (1901). 'Yá-Bahá'u'l-Abhá' is an Arabic invocation which literally means 'O Thou the Glory of the Most Glorious', a reference to Bahá'u'lláh Who, according to His followers, is the Glory of God for this day. See http://bahai-library.com/breakwell_hopper_brittingham.
31. *Bahá'í Prayers*, p. 59.
32. Bahá'u'lláh, *Prayers and Meditations*, CXXXV, p. 223.
33. *Bahá'í Prayers*, p. 73.

10 Metta Meditation

1. Bahá'u'lláh, *Hidden Words*, Persian no. 3.
2. The language of many of the earlist extant Buddhist scriptures.
3. Salzberg, *Loving-kindness: The Revolutionary Art of Happiness*, p. 18.
4. ibid. p. 21.
5. ibid. p. 23.
6. ibid. pp. 29–31.
7. Shapiro and Shapiro, *The Meditation Book*, p. 40.
8. Shapiro and Shapiro, *Peace Within the Stillness*, p. 165.
9. Shapiro and Shapiro, *The Meditation Book*, p. 40.
10. ibid. p. 41.
11. Davich, *The Best Guide to Meditation*, pp. 273–91.
12. Newberg and Waldman, *How God Changes Your Brain*, pp. 208–9.
13. Walsh, *Essential Spirituality*, p. 102.
14. Bahá'u'lláh, *Hidden Words*, Persian no. 56.
15. 'Abdu'l-Bahá, *Selections from the Writings of 'Abdu'l-Bahá*, no. 225, p. 294.
16. 'Abdu'l-Bahá, *Paris Talks*, ch. 6, p. 19.
17. 'Abdu'l-Bahá, *'Abdu'l-Bahá in London*, p. 79.
18. 'Abdu'l-Bahá, *Paris Talks*, ch. 58, pp. 193–4.
19. ibid. ch. 1, p. 2.
20. 'Abdu'l-Bahá, *The Promulgation of Universal Peace*, p. 9.
21. Bahá'u'lláh, *Tablets of Bahá'u'lláh Revealed after the Kitáb-i-Aqdas*, p. 161.

11 Mantra Meditation (Japa Meditation)

1. Easwaran, *The Mantram Handbook*, p. 8.
2. ibid. p. 32.
3. Leloup, *Being Still: Reflections on an Ancient Mystical Tradition*, p. 96.
4. Shapiro and Shapiro, *The Meditation Book*, p. 62.
5. Shapiro and Shapiro, *Meditation for Inner Peace*, p. 159.
6. 'Amida' or 'Amita' is the Japanese form of the two Sanskrit names of a Buddha: Amitabha (Limitless Light) and Amitayus (Limitless Life).
7. The Zohar (Hebrew: Splendour or Radiance) is a collection of commentaries in the literature of Jewish mystical thought known as Kabbalah. According to Kabbalist beliefs, the Zohar is intended for those who have already attained spiritual perception.
8. Hebrew, literally 'divorced from the world'.
9. Kaplan, *Jewish Meditation*, pp. 57–8.
10. Davich, *The Best Guide to Meditation*, pp. 156–8.
11. Reininger, *Centering Prayer in Daily Life and Ministry*, p. 130.

12. ibid. p. 131.
13. *Zikr*: short for *dhikrullah*, Arabic, literally 'making mention of God'.
14. Scholl, 'The Remembrance of God'.
15. Goleman, *The Meditative Mind*, p. 55.
16. See for example Qur'án 20:124; 43:36; 33:41–42; 13:28; 18:28; 29:45; 2:152; 24:37; 7:205; 57:16; 63:9; 5:91; 26:227; 73:8; 5:91.
17. Kabbani, *The Naqshbandi Sufi Tradition Guidebook of Daily Practices and Devotions*, p. 108.
18. ibid. p. 95.
19. Isaiah 26:3.
20. Devananda, *Meditation and Mantras*, p. 78.
21. Gillet, *On the Invocation of the Name of Jesus*, pp. 19, 21.
22. Leloup, *Being Still: Reflections on an Ancient Mystical Tradition*, p. 3.
23. Reported words of 'Abdu'l-Bahá, in Esslemont, *Bahá'u'lláh and the New Era*. See the compilation *Prayer, Meditation and the Devotional Attitude*, in *The Compilation of Compilations*, vol. II, no. 1756.
24. Shapiro and Shapiro, *The Meditation Book*, p. 62.
25. Kabbani, *The Naqshbandi Sufi Tradition*, p. 52.
26. Qur'án 20:42.
27. Easwaran, *The Mantram Handbook*, pp. 61–2.
28. ibid. p. 9.
29. ibid. p. 91.
30. Devananda, *Meditation and Mantras*, p. 80.
31. Mataji, *Nama Japa*, p. 122.
32. ibid. p. 231.
33. Dass, *Journey of Awakening*, p. 54.
34. Makarios and Nicodemus, *Writings from the Philokalia on Prayer of the Heart*, pp. 223, 288.
35. Quoted in 'Dhikr: Remembrance of God'.
36. Bahá'u'lláh, *Prayers and Meditations*, CXXII, p. 208.
37. Bhagavad Gita 8:14.
38. Prov. 18:10.
39. Psalms 54:1.
40. Col. 3:17.
41. John 14:13–14.
42. Qur'án 87:14–15.
43. Bahá'u'lláh, *Prayers and Meditations*, LV, p. 78.
44. ibid. CLXX, p. 262.
45. 'Abdu'l-Bahá, 'Tablet of the Greatest Name', unpublished authorized translation, see note 67 below.
46. *Bahá'í Prayers*, p. 27.

47. Bahá'u'lláh, *Prayers and Meditations*, LXXIV, p. 122.
48. ibid. CLXXIX, p. 304.
49. Literally, the name of Rama, a Hindu deity.
50. Rahim is an Arabic word meaning 'The Most Merciful'. In Islam, Rahim is considered to be one of the 99 attributes of Allah (God). The use of Rahim here also shows Gandhi's respect for other religious belief systems.
51. Gandhi, *Prayer*, p. 169.
52. Gandhi, *Ramanama*, p. 13.
53. ibid.
54. ibid.
55. Deshpande (ed.), *The Way to God: Selected Writings from Mahatma Gandhi*, pp. 58–9.
56. Gandhi, *Ramanama*, p. 30.
57. ibid. p. 44.
58. De Mello, *Contact with God*, p. 90.
59. Bahá'u'lláh, *Epistle to the Son of the Wolf*, p. 128.
60. Lambden, 'The Word Bahá: Quintessence of the Greatest Name'.
61. Lambden, 'The Du'á Saḥar'.
62. Lambden, 'The Word Bahá'.
63. Momen, 'The Concept of Light in Iranian Religion'.
64. Lambden, 'The Greatest Name'.
65. Letter on behalf of Shoghi Effendi to the National Spiritual Assembly of Australia and New Zealand, 26 December 1941, in Shoghi Effendi, *Letters from the Guardian to Australia and New Zealand 1923–1957*, p. 41.
66. Letter written on behalf of Shoghi Effendi to the National Spiritual Assembly of the United States and Canada, 28 April 1935, in *Bahá'í News*, No. 93, p. 1, July 1935. Quoted in *Lights of Guidance*, no. 911, p. 270.
67. 'Abdu'l-Bahá, 'Tablet of the Greatest Name'. The Universal House of Justice comments: 'The passage is taken from an unpublished authorized translation of a Tablet of 'Abdu'l-Bahá.'
68. Lambden, 'The Word Bahá'.
69. ibid.
70. 'Abdu'l-Bahá, quoted in *Lights of Guidance*, no. 892, p. 266.
71. Provisional translation by Farnaz and Bijan Masumian; original Persian:

اليوم، رداء افعال و اكليل اعمال، ذكر اسم اعظم در
ظاهر و باطن بوده. (امر و خلق جلد ٣، ص ۴۴۴)

72. Breakwell et al., *Utterances of our Blessed Master*, p. 10.
73. *Bahá'í Writings on Some Aspects of Health, Healing, Nutrition and*

Related Matters, in *The Compilation of Compilations*, vol. 1, no. 1015, p. 459.

74. ibid. no. 1025, p. 460.
75. 'Abdu'l-Bahá, *Tablets of Abdul-Baha Abbas*, vol. 3, p. 629.
76. 'Abdu'l-Bahá, quoted in *Lights of Guidance*, no. 892, p. 266.
77. Bahá'u'lláh, *The Kitáb-i-Aqdas*, para. 132, p. 66.
78. *Bahá'í Prayers*, p. 33.
79. 'Abdu'l-Bahá, 'Tablet of the Greatest Name'.
80. ibid.
81. Provisional translation by Farnaz and Bijan Masumian; original Arabic:

كلّما احاطتنا الرزايا دفعناه باسم ربك العلي العظيم . (كتاب مبين، ص ٤٥١)

82. 'Abdu'l-Bahá, quoted in *Lights of Guidance,* no. 892, p. 266.
83. 'Abdu'l-Bahá, *Tablets of Abdul-Baha Abbas*, vol. 3, p. 713.
84. 'Abdu'l-Bahá, 'Tablet of the Greatest Name'.
85. 'Abdu'l-Bahá, *Tablets of Abdul-Baha Abbas*, vol. 3, p. 674.
86. 'Abdu'l-Bahá, 'Tablet of the Greatest Name'.
87. ibid.
88. Bahá'u'lláh, *Prayers and Meditations*, CLXXIX, p. 307.
89. 'Abdu'l-Bahá, 'Tablet of the Greatest Name'.
90. Bahá'u'lláh, *The Kitáb-i-Aqdas*, para. 51, p. 38.
91. 'Abdu'l-Bahá, quoted in *Lights of Guidance*, no. 892, p. 266.
92. ibid.
93. 'Abdu'l-Bahá, *Tablets of Abdul-Baha Abbas,* vol. 3, p. 674.
94. Bahá'u'lláh, *Prayers and Meditations*, LXV, pp. 103–4.
95. Bahá'u'lláh, 'Tablet of Medicine', provisional translation.
96. Literally, 'repeating in written form'.
97. Devananda, *Meditation and Mantras*, pp. 80–81.
98. Vandana, *Nama Japa*, p. 29.
99. ibid.

12 Gratitude Meditation

1. 'Abdu'l-Bahá, *Tablets of Abdul-Baha Abbas*, vol. 2, p. 483.
2. Popov, *The Family Virtues Guide*, p. 50.
3. Sanders, *Today We are Rich*, pp. 131–2.
4. ibid. p. 112.
5. Emmons, *Thanks! How the New Science of Gratitude Can Make You Happier*, p. 11.
6. ibid. p. 36.
7. Carnegie, *How to Stop Worrying and Start Living*, p. 142.
8. Emmons, *Thanks!*, p. 76.
9. ibid. p. 189.

10. Samovar: Russian, literally 'self-boiler', a heated metal container used in Russia and other parts of Europe as well as in the Middle East to heat and boil water, typically for making tea.
11. 'Abdu'l-Bahá, *Memorials of the Faithful*, p. 25.
12. Bahá'u'lláh, *Tablets of Bahá'u'lláh Revealed after the Kitáb-i-Aqdas*, p. 26.
13. ibid. p. 156.
14. 'Abdu'l-Bahá, *The Promulgation of Universal Peace*, p. 51.
15. Bahá'u'lláh, *Ad'íyiy-i-Ḥaḍrat-i Maḥbúb*, pp. 49–52. Authorised translation, letter from the Universal House of Justice to a local Spiritual Assembly, 5 May 2014.
16. Qur'án 2:172.
17. Anguttara Nikaya i: 61, quoted in Wilson, *World Scripture*, p. 556.
18. Qur'án 40:61, 64.

13 Music Meditation

1. 'Abdu'l-Bahá, in *Music*, in *The Compilation of Compilations*, vol. 2, no. 1421.
2. Bahá'u'lláh, *The Kitáb-i-Aqdas*, para. 51, p. 38.
3. 'Abdu'l-Bahá, *The Promulgation of Universal Peace*, p. 52.
4. 'Abdu'l-Bahá, *Selections from the Writings of 'Abdu'l-Bahá*, no. 74, p. 112.
5. 'Abdu'l-Bahá, quoted in Zarqání, *Maḥmúd's Diary*, p. 204.
6. 'Abdu'l-Bahá, as quoted in Lucas, *A Brief Account of My Visit to Acca*, p. 14.

14 Contemplation or Reflection on the Word of God

1. Bahá'u'lláh, Lawḥ-i-Ḥikmat, in *Tablets of Bahá'u'lláh Revealed after the Kitáb-i-Aqdas*, p. 143.
2. Bahá'u'lláh, *Gleanings*, LXX, p. 136.
3. ibid. LXXIX, p. 152.
4. Literally 'physician' or 'wise one'.
5 Bahá'u'lláh, *Gleanings*, XCIX, p. 200.
6. ibid. LXXIV, p. 141.
7. Bahá'u'lláh, Lawḥ-i-Dunyá, in *Tablets of Bahá'u'lláh Revealed after the Kitáb-i-Aqdas*, p. 89; also in *Gleanings*, XLIII, p. 96.
8. ibid. CLXII, p. 342.
9. Joshua 1:8.
10. Letter on behalf of Shoghi Effendi to an individual believer, 15 October 1952, in *Lights of Guidance*, no. 381, p. 112.
11. 'Abdu'l-Bahá, *'Abdu'l-Bahá in London*, p. 80.
12. The Báb, Persian Bayán IX:10, in *Selections from the Writings of the Báb*, p. 99.

13. Bahá'u'lláh, The Kitáb-i-Aqdas, para 149, p. 73.
14. 'Abdu'l-Bahá, Selections from the Writings of 'Abdu'l-Bahá, no. 17, p. 35.
15. Quoted in Honnold, Vignettes from the Life of 'Abdu'l-Bahá, p. 49, from Thompson, Diary, p. 387.
16. 'Abdu'l-Bahá, The Promulgation of Universal Peace, pp. 459–60.
17. See' Abdu'l-Bahá, Paris Talks, p. 49: 'Let us ask God's help to enable us to understand the Holy Books.'
18. Bahá'u'lláh, Hidden Words, Arabic no. 31.
19. 'Abdu'l-Bahá, Paris Talks, ch. 23, p. 68.
20. Attributed to 'Abdu'l-Bahá, Star of the West, vol. 9, no. 8, p. 96.
21. Walsh, Essential Spirituality, p. 239.
22. Bahá'u'lláh, Lawḥ-i-Ḥikmat, in Tablets of Bahá'u'lláh Revealed after the Kitáb-i-Aqdas, p. 138.
23. Dhammapada 18:239.
24. 'Abdu'l-Bahá, Selections from the Writings of 'Abdu'l-Bahá, no. 86, p. 118.
25. ibid. no. 92, p. 122.

15 Passages for Contemplation

1. Bahá'u'lláh, The Tabernacle of Unity, p. 28.
2. Bhagavad Gita 3:30–32.
3. ibid. 3:20.
4. ibid. 3:21.
5. ibid. 9:31.
6. ibid. 12:13–14.
7. ibid. 12:15–20.
8. Dhammapada 1:1.
9. ibid. 1:3–8. Mara is the demon that tempted Gautama Buddha.
10. ibid. 23:327.
11. ibid. 18:236.
12. ibid. 16:219–22.
13. ibid. 11:151.
14. ibid. 9:12.
15. ibid. 6:89.
16. ibid. 5:62.
17. ibid. 4:53.
18. Deut. 6:4–7.
19. Psalms 1:1–3.
20. ibid. 18:2.
21. ibid. 27:14.
22. ibid. 26:1.
23. ibid. 27:4.

24. ibid. 34:1.
25. ibid. 34:8.
26. ibid. 34:19.
27. ibid. 39:6.
28. ibid. 73:25–26.
29. ibid. 91:14–15.
30. Prov. 8:17.
31. ibid. 27:1–2.
32. ibid. 29:25.
33. Matt. 5:1–12.
34. ibid. 6:19–21.
35. ibid. 7:1.
36. ibid. 7:3–4.
37. ibid. 7:7–8.
38. ibid. 5:38, 39, 43–6.
39. Gal. 6:9.
40. 1 Thess. 5:14.
41. Qur'án 2:177.
42. ibid. 2:110.
43. ibid. 2:186.
44. ibid. 3:142.
45. ibid. 6:162.
46. ibid. 16:95–6.
47. ibid. 49:12.
48. ibid. 50:16.
49. ibid. 65:7.
50. ibid. 65:3.
51. ibid. 94:5.
52. Bahá'u'lláh, *The Seven Valleys*, pp. 21–2.
53. Bahá'u'lláh, *Gleanings*, CXXX, p. 285.
54. 'Abdu'l-Bahá, *Selections from the Writings of 'Abdu'l-Bahá*, no. 1, p. 3.
55. Bahá'u'lláh, *Gleanings*, CLIII, pp. 326–9.
56. ibid. CXXIV, p. 262.
57. 'Abdu'l-Bahá, *The Promulgation of Universal Peace*, p. 148.
58. ibid. pp. 335–6.
59. Bahá'u'lláh, *Gleanings*, CXVII, p. 250.
60. 'Abdu'l-Bahá, *The Promulgation of Universal Peace*, pp. 226–7.
61. 'Abdu'l-Bahá, *Selections from the Writings of 'Abdu'l-Bahá*, no. 176, pp. 204–5.
62. Bahá'u'lláh, *The Tabernacle of Unity*, p. 41.
63. Reported words of 'Abdu'l-Bahá, in Maxwell, *An Early Pilgrimage*, pp. 20–21.
64. Bahá'u'lláh, *The Summons of the Lord of Hosts*, p. 109.

65. ibid. p. 202.
66. 'Abdu'l-Bahá, *Tablets*, vol. III, pp. 709–10.
67. Bahá'u'lláh, *Epistle to the Son of the Wolf*, p. 132.
68. 'Abdu'l-Bahá, *The Promulgation of Universal Peace*, p. 147.
69. Bahá'u'lláh, *Gleanings*, CXXXVII, p. 299.
70. 'Abdu'l-Bahá, *Paris Talks*, no. 26, p. 78.
71. Bahá'u'lláh, *Epistle to the Son of the Wolf*, p. 56.
72. Bahá'u'lláh, *Gleanings*, CXXIII, p. 261.
73. 'Abdu'l-Bahá, *Selections from the Writings of 'Abdu'l-Bahá*, no. 156, p. 185.
74. Bahá'u'lláh, *The Tabernacle of Unity*, p. 9; also in *Tablets*, p. 169.
75. Bahá'u'lláh, *The Summons of the Lord of Hosts*, pp. 109–10.
76. ibid. p. 150.
77. ibid. p. 154.
78. ibid. pp. 190–91.
79. ibid. p. 208.
80. 'Abdu'l-Bahá, *The Secret of Divine Civilization*, p. 19.
81. Bahá'u'lláh, *Tablets of Bahá'u'lláh Revealed after the Kitáb-i-Aqdas*, pp. 153–7.

16 Healing Meditation

1. 'Abdu'l-Bahá, *Tablets*, vol. III, p. 654.
2. ibid. vol. II, p. 309.
3. Gawler, *Peace of Mind*, p. 168.
4. Thondup, *The Healing Power of Mind*, p. 106.
5. ibid. p. 95.
6. ibid. p. 97.
7. Bahá'u'lláh, *The Seven Valleys*, p. 39.
8. Momen, 'The Concept of Light in Iranian Religion'.
9. Masumian and Masumian, *Divine Educators*, p. 54.
10. Momen, 'The Concept of Light in Iranian Religion'.
11. Bhagavad Gita 13:17.
12. ibid. 8:9–10.
13. ibid. 10:12.
14. ibid.11:12.
15. ibid. 13:33.
16. *Arjuna*: Sanskrit word meaning 'bright' or 'shining'. In Hindu mythology, Arjuna is a great warrior, the hero of the Hindu epic Mahabharata. The conversations between Arjuna and Krishna are the centrepiece of the Bhagavad Gita (Song of the Lord) which is one of the most popular Hindu sacred texts.
17. Bhagavad Gita 11:47.
18. ibid. 15:12.

19. Momen, *Buddhism and the Bahá'í Faith*, p. 36.
20. Psalms 27:1.
21. ibid. 119:105.
22. Prov. 6:23.
23. Isaiah 60:19–20.
24. Shechinah: The presence of God on earth or a symbol or manifestation of His presence.
25. Pinson, *Meditation and Judaism*, p. 130.
26. James 1:17.
27. 1 John 1:5.
28. John 1:6–10.
29. ibid. 3:19.
30. 2 Cor. 4:6.
31. Rev. 21:23.
32. John 9:5.
33. ibid. 12:46.
34. ibid. 8:12.
35. ibid. 12:35–6.
36. Qur'án 24:35.
37. ibid. 4:174.
38. ibid. 61:8.
39. ibid. 7:157.
40. ibid. 64:8.
41. ibid. 42:52.
42. ibid. 5:15–18.
43. Helminski, *Women of Sufism*, p. 116.
44. ibid.
45. Momen, 'The Concept of Light in Iranian Religion'.
46. ibid.
47. ibid.
48. The Báb, *Selections from the Writings of the Báb*, p. 74.
49. ibid. pp. 154–5.
50. ibid. p. 103.
51. Bahá'u'lláh, *Prayers and Meditations*, CLXXVI, pp. 269–70.
52. Bahá'u'lláh, *Gleanings from the Writings of Bahá'u'lláh*. XC, p. 177.
53. Bahá'u'lláh, *Prayers and Meditations*, III, pp. 5–6.
54. Bahá'u'lláh, Obligatory Prayer, in most Bahá'í prayer books, also in *Prayers and Meditations*, CLXXXII, p. 314.
55. Quoted by Bahá'u'lláh, *Gems of Divine Mysteries*, p. 31.
56. Bahá'u'lláh, *Prayers and Meditations*, X, p. 13.
57. 'Abdu'l-Bahá, *Paris Talks*, no. 36, p. 114.
58. Bahá'u'lláh, in *Bahá'í Prayers*, p. 148.
59. Bahá'u'lláh, 'Tablet of All Food'.

60. Bahá'u'lláh, *Tablets of Bahá'u'lláh Revealed after the Kitáb-i-Aqdas*, p. 33.
61. ibid. p. 119
62. ibid. p. 14.
63. ibid. p. 13.
64. Bahá'u'lláh, *Prayers and Meditations*, IX, p. 12.
65. 'Abdu'l-Bahá, *Memorials of the Faithful*, p. 171.
66. Bahá'u'lláh, *The Summons of the Lord of Hosts*, p. 68.
67. Bahá'u'lláh, *Tablets of Bahá'u'lláh Revealed after the Kitáb-i-Aqdas*, p. 102.
68. ibid. p. 108.
69. Bahá'u'lláh, *The Kitáb-i-Aqdas*, para. 85, p. 50.
70. Bahá'u'lláh, *Prayers and Meditations*, LXXIX, p. 130.
71. Moody, *Life After Life*, p. 8. For a thorough discussion of alternative theories about NDEs and responses to them by NDE experts, see Holden, Greyson and James, *The Handbook of Near-Death Experiences: Thirty Years of Investigation.*
72. Masumian, *Life After Death*, p. 125.
73. 'Abdu'l-Bahá, *Memorials of the Faithful*, p. 47.
74. ibid. p. 75.
75. Quoted in Masumian, *Life After Death,* p. 140.
76. ibid. p. 125.

17 Visualization

1. Prov. 29:18.
2. Newberg and Waldman, *How God Changes Your Brain*, p. 188.
3. Samuels and Samuels, *Healing with the Mind's Eye*, pp. 73–4.
4. Shapiro and Shapiro, *Peace Within the Stillness*, p. 101.
5. ibid. pp. 104–5.
6. Brother Lawrence. *The Practice of the Presence of God,* p. 58.
7. Psalms 16:11.
8. Shapiro and Shapiro, *Meditation for Inner Peace*, p. 100.
9. Moen, *Meditations for Healing*, pp. 123–4.
10. Matt. 17:20.
11. Gawain, *Creative Visualization*, pp. 24–5.
12. Newberg and Waldman, *How God Changes Your Brain*, p. 167.
13. Gawain, *Creative Visualization*, p. 17.
14. Webster, *Creative Visualization for Beginners*, p. 66.
15. ibid. p. 64.
16. ibid. pp. 65–6.

18 Daily Meditation and Visualization

1. Bahá'u'lláh, in *Bahá'í Prayers*, p. 73.

2. Bahá'u'lláh, *The Four Valleys*, p. 63.
3. Bahá'u'lláh, *The Summons of the Lord of Hosts*, p. 133.
4. Bahá'u'lláh, *Prayers and Meditations*, CXXVII, p. 214.
5. ibid. LXXXV, p. 144.
6. Bahá'u'lláh, *Hidden Words*, Persian no. 4.
7. Psalms 46:10.
8. 'When a man observes the wafting of the breeze among these trees, he hears the rustling of the leaves and sees the swaying of the trees, it is as though all are praising and acknowledging the one true God' ('Abdu'l-Bahá, quoted in Zarqání, *Maḥmúd's Diary*, p. 192).
9. Bahá'u'lláh, *Prayers and Meditations*, CVII, p. 178.
10. 'Guide my steps, O my God, unto that which is acceptable and pleasing to Thee' (The Báb, in *Bahá'í Prayers*, p. 131).
11. '. . . hold me back from entering habitations not desired by Thee' (ibid.).
12. 'It [The Greatest Name] should be fed upon by constant use in daily invocations, in trouble, under opposition . . . It is the name of comfort, protection . . .' (Lambden, 'The Word Bahá: Quintessence of the Greatest Name').
13. Bahá'u'lláh, *Prayers and Meditations*, CXXVI, p. 213.
14. The Báb, in *Bahá'í Prayers*, p. 128.
15. Bahá'u'lláh, *Tabernacle of Unity*, p. 50.
16. 'O my God, my Master, the Goal of my desire! This, Thy servant, seeketh to sleep in the shelter of Thy mercy, and to repose beneath the canopy of Thy grace, imploring Thy care and Thy protection' (Bahá'u'lláh, in *Bahá'í Prayers*, p. 59).
17. ibid. p. 148.
18. ibid. p. 60.
19. Bahá'u'lláh, *The Summons of the Lord of Hosts*, p. 150.
20. Bahá'u'lláh, *Gleanings from the Writings of Bahá'u'lláh*, XLIII, p. 94; also in *Tablets*, p. 87.
21. Bahá'u'lláh, *The Seven Valleys*, p. 5.
22. Qur'án 41:35.
23. ibid. 7:201.
24. Bahá'u'lláh, *Hidden Words*, Arabic no. 36.
25. Hanh, *Being Peace*, p. 9.
26. Lewis, *Free Your Breath, Free Your Life*, p. 60.
27. Newberg and Waldman, *How God Changes Your Brain*, p. 151.
28. Klein, *Healing Power of Humor*, p. 96.
29. ibid. p. 97.
30. ibid. p. 99.
31. Hanh, *Peace Is Every Step*, pp. 6–7.
32. Prov. 17:22.

33. Dhammapada, 15:199–200.
34. Psalms 32:11.
35. Prov. 15:13.
36. Phil. 4:4.
37. Psalms 16:8–11.
38. Bahá'u'lláh, *Gleanings*, CXLVII, p. 316.
39. ibid. CXXX, p. 285.
40 'Abdu'l-Bahá, as reported in Zarqání, *Maḥmúd's Diary*, p. 139.
41. Bahá'u'lláh, *The Kitáb-i-Aqdas*, para. 132, p. 66.
42. Lewis, *Free Your Breath, Free Your Life*, p. 66.
43. Bahá'u'lláh, in *The Compilation of Compilations*, vol. 1, no. 1020, p. 460.
44. Bahá'u'lláh, *The Tabernacle of Unity*, p. 8.
45. Popov, *The Family Virtues Guide*, p. 251.
46. 'Abdu'l-Bahá, *The Promulgation of Universal Peace*, p. 244.
47. Bahá'u'lláh, *Hidden Words*, Persian no. 3.
48. Gauding, *The Meditation Bible*.

19 An Angel for the Day

1. 'Abdu'l-Bahá, *Selections from the Writings of 'Abdu'l-Bahá*, no. 39, p. 81.
2. ibid. no. 142, p. 166.
3. Bahá'u'lláh, *Majmuih-yi-Alvah-i-Mubarikih*, provisional translation by Farnaz and Bijan Masumian with assistance from Dr Omid Ghaemmaghami:
4. The Báb, *Selections from the Writings of the Báb*, pp. 192–3.
5. Qur'án 33:43.
6. ibid. 13:11.

جميع شما اشجار رضوان قدس منيد كه بدست مرحمت خود در ارض مباركه غرس فرمودم و بنيسان رحمت بى‌زوال خود تربيت نمودم و از حوادث كونيّه و خطرات ملكيّه بملائك حفظيّه حفظ فرمودم. (مجموعة الواح مبارك، ص ٣١٩)

7. ibid. 86:4.
8. Psalms 91:9–12.
9. Hebr. 1:14.
10. 'Abdu'l-Bahá, *Tablets*, vol. II, p. 446.
11. 'Abdu'l-Bahá, *Selections from the Writings of 'Abdu'l-Bahá*, no. 2, p. 6.
12. Bahá'u'lláh, *The Kitáb-i-Aqdas*, para. 53, p. 39.
13. 'Abdu'l-Bahá, *Tablets*, vol. I, p. 145–6.
14. 'Abdu'l-Bahá, *Selections from the Writings of 'Abdu'l-Bahá*, no. 142, p. 165.
15. 'Abdu'l-Bahá, *The Promulgation of Universal Peace*, p. 7.

16. 'Abdu'l-Bahá, *Tablets*, vol. III, p. 554.
17. Bahá'u'lláh, *The Seven Valleys*, p. 17.
18. Zarqání, *Badáyi'u'l-Áthár*. vol. 2, p. 107. The original Persian tribute is

    او عبارت از نفس من است. (بدايع الاثار جلد ٢، ص ١٠٧

19. 'Abdu'l-Bahá, *Memorials of the Faithful*, p. xi.
20. ibid. p. 190.
21. Root, *Ṭáhirih the Pure*, pp. 5–6; quoted from Esslemont, *Bahá'u'lláh and the New Era*, pp. 147–8.
22. ibid. p. 40.
23. 'Abdu'l-Bahá, *Memorials of the Faithful*, p. 101.
24. ibid. p. 43.
25. ibid. pp. 48–9.
26. ibid. pp. 41–2.
27. 'Abdu'l-Bahá, *Paris Talks*, ch. 57, p. 192.
28. 'Abdu'l-Bahá, *'Abdu'l-Bahá in London*, p. 96.

DIVINE EDUCATORS

by Farnaz Ma'súmián and Bijan Ma'súmián

Continued religious strife in different parts of the world, the rise of militancy and global terrorism have put the need for dialogue at the top of many government agendas. In a world where terrorism has led to misunderstandings about the true nature of religion, many people are either becoming entrenched in religious fundamentalism of one kind or another, or are turning away from religion altogether. Both are a tragedy, leaving millions worldwide without access to the spiritual heritage of humanity.

But other signs point to a brighter future in the dawn of an 'ecumenical age', and in the growing acceptance of religious pluralism as a sign of social civility worldwide.

In writing *Divine Educators*, Farnaz and Bijan Ma'súmián have been not only spurred on by the current crisis in religious prejudice, but also encouraged by the increasing realization that despite diverse, sometimes conflicting, cultural expressions and human interpretations, all the great religious traditions of the world share a common foundation that fosters love, unity, and brotherhood.

This book provides scriptural and historical evidence for commonalities in the lives, characters, and teachings of the central figures of seven world religions: Hinduism, Buddhism, Zoroastrianism, Judaism, Christianity, Islam and the Bahá'í Faith, from the sources of each religious tradition, including the Bhagavad Gita, the Dhammapadha, the Gathas, the Hebrew Bible, the Gospels, the Qur'án and the Writings of Bahá'u'lláh. It is bound to generate interest in the subject and further the cause of interfaith dialogue and understanding throughout the world.

ISBN: 978-0-85398-499-3
176 pages, 210 x 138 mm (8.5 x 5.5 ins)

THE CALM HANDBOOK

by Paul Profaska

Many people today are interested in meditation and its benefits but do not know how to start. This is an easy-to-follow course designed for small groups of beginners. No particular form of meditation is promoted but the course, which is based on the Bahá'í writings, introduces participants to reflection on scripture in a gentle and profound way, and it generates strong bonds of fellowship amongst group members.

The CALM course is designed for small groups of beginners who are initially guided through the meditation by a Coordinator. The *CALM Coordinator's Guide: A Communal Approach to Learning* provides an easy to follow, step by step guidebook that will help new Coordinators start CALM courses and assist them to take learners through the rudiments of meditation to the ability to meditate on their own.

The CALM course helps us :
- open our hearts and minds to the spiritual reserves that lie within us all, such as love, insight, calmness, courage and enthusiasm
- explore the principles of meditation
- practise meditation skills
- develop our own practice
- and shows us how meditation can be applied in our lives.

Comes complete with the CALM Guided Meditation CD.

ISBN: 978-0-85398-493-1
96 pages   29.7 x 21 cm (11.75 x 8.25 ins)

MEDITATION

by Wendi Momen

In many places in the Bahá'í writings we are to 'meditate upon this', 'to ponder', 'to reflect'. Meditation is one of the six essential requisites for our spiritual growth. It is one of the purposes of the Bahá'í fast. Through meditation 'the doors of deeper knowledge and inspiration' are opened.

Such an important feature of life surely merits development. However, many of us do not know what meditation is or how to go about it. This book uses the Bahá'í scriptures as the focus for meditation. It briefly describes a number of techniques and practices that one might employ to develop this faculty and provides verses from the Bahá'í writings upon which to meditate.

ISBN: 978-0-85398-407-8
144 pages
17.8 x 11.0 cm (7 x 4.25 in)

Information about all other George Ronald titles can be found at

www.grbooks.com